SOLILOQUY!

THE SHAKESPEARE MONOLOGUES
(Women)

by William Shakespeare

Edited by Michael Earley & Philippa Keil

APPLAUSE
THEATRE BOOK PUBLISHERS

SOLILOQUY! THE SHAKESPEARE MONOLOGUES (women)
Copyright © 1988 by Applause Theatre Book Publishers
Introduction and Commentaries copyright © 1988 by Michael Earley

Library of Congress Cataloging-in-Publication Data

Shakespeare, William, 1564–1616.
  Soliloquy!: the Shakespeare monologues (women).

  (The Applause acting series)
  Bibliography: p.
  1. Monologues. 2. Acting. I. Earley, Michael. II. Keil, Philippa
III. Title. IV. Title: Monologues (women) V. Series.
PR2771.E153 1988 822'.3'3 87-33500
ISBN 0-936839-79-1

Applause Theatre Book Publishers
211 West 71Street, New York, NY 10023
phone: (212) 595-4735 • fax: (212) 721-2856

Cover photo: Sara Bernhardt in the role of Hamlet courtesy of
              Mitchenson and Mander Theatre Collection, London.

TABLE OF CONTENTS

iv

ON ACTING SHAKESPEARE

Michael Earley

Performing a speech by Shakespeare—in an audition, rehearsal, or production—is one of the touchstone experiences of the stage. *Every* actor, no matter how experienced or confident, in the very act of mouthing the frequently quoted lines in this volume, immediately senses an instant frisson from the ghostly presence of "others": the voice prints and patterns of countless preceeding actors who have also confronted the same speeches and stamped their own personalities on the very same lines. They are not just the great "stars," like Laurence Olivier and Sarah Bernhardt who grace the covers of the men's and women's editions of *Soliloquy!*, but tens of thousands of lesser lights equally struck and captivated by the luminescence of Shakespeare's characters and his dramatic language. Like the actor looking at these speeches for the first time, like you, every past performer has picked his or her way through the same process and has wrestled with the same acting problems: how to speak the verse, how to give body and weight to character, how to communicate complex thoughts smoothly, how to sustain a long speech with ease and interest. Few traditions in the theatre that bind actors together are as common as this one. Is it any wonder that all actors, especially young ones, approach Shakespeare's soliloquies with awe, fear, and trepidation?

Yes, the Shakespeare monologues do have a reverential and monumental quality about them. They seem more *quotable* than *actable*. And they certainly are daunting histrionic challenges; deceptively natural and realistic at times, heightened and stylized at other points. Yet Shakespeare's speeches are meant to be acted and not just quoted. He never lets you forget that you are an actor on a platform stage performing. Only when the speeches are lifted off the page and become onstage events do their power, potential, and infinite variety spring to life.

It always amazes me how the *fear* of doing Shakespeare is so easily replaced by the *ease* of performing Shakespeare once actors are on their feet with the text, setting the words and ideas in motion. Without fail the speeches offer their own guidance and direction. For Shakespeare, better than any dramatist before or since, gives an actor everything he or she needs in order to do the work: clear motivations and intentions, expressive moods and emotions, precise stresses and phrasings. How he does this, and how any actor can begin probing the texts on his or her own for some of these cues, is what I want to focus on here. The "Commentaries" that follow each of the monologues in this volume continue these observations on a speech by speech basis. So let's set the stage for acting Shakespeare.

We have all been taught the same basic lesson: William Shakespeare (1564-1616) was a writer without peer. Who would even dare dispute that claim? What we have failed to learn, because it is so quickly glossed over, is the fact that Shakespeare began, continued, and ended his career in the theatre as an *actor*. His playwriting career grew out of his acting efforts, and he practiced both professions simultaneously until he retired from the theatre around 1613. Not only did he perform in his own plays (although no one is quite sure about which roles) and those of others (we do know he appeared in ones by Ben Jonson), he was also an active and principal shareholder in the best English acting company of his day: the Lord Chamberlain's Men, later called the King's Men.

When Shakespeare began to write plays, he wrote them for actors like himself. No thought was given to publishing his dramas. First editions came mainly after his death. Shakespeare's interests were fixed firmly on the stage, actors, and an audience of listeners. Just imagine for a moment, being one of those actors in the Chamberlain's/ King's Men, grappling *for the first time* with one of Shakespeare's freshly minted texts and, under the pressure and heat of a hastily rehearsed production, helping the author polish his lines to a glistening sheen of perfection. The working relationship between playwright and player must have been the same then as it still is today when dramatists and actors collaborate on a new play.

What Shakespeare must have kept squarely in mind, as he wrote his two and sometimes three plays a year, was the fact that he was writing for an actor's theatre. It was actors, after all, *not* plays, whom Elizabethan audiences flocked across the Thames to see at the Globe and other theatres which dotted London's south bank. Directors had no part in the process because they, as a profession, did not yet even exist. The art of the performer was the central focus in everyone's mind. Richard Burbage, who joined the Chamberlain's Men about the same time as Shakespeare, added to the playwright's vision by his handling of the very first performances of Richard III, Hamlet, Othello, Macbeth, and King Lear. His markings and expressive powers as an actor must certainly have found their way into the texts. And Burbage must have been just one of the many actors who inspired Shakespeare. The apprentice boy actors, still unknown to us by names, but thought to be uncommonly good performers, have equally left their traces on the great female roles: Rosalind, Beatrice, Juliet, Cleopatra, Ophelia, Desdemona, Lady Macbeth, and Lear's daughters. This kind of speculation should lead us out of the labyrinth of literary thinking by returning us to the stage and the craft of actors.

As a writer, and certainly as a performer, Shakespeare was in love with the image of acting. His characters are forever conscious of playing "roles." When faced with the reality of suicide his Juliet says, "My dismal scene I needs must act alone" (4.3.19). His Mark Antony is so skillful at manipulating a rough crowd at the funeral of Julius Caesar because he is a lover of good oratory and acting techniques. Speech after speech in Shakespeare hinges on the metaphor of theatre. Think, for instance, of the most blatant one by Jaques in *As You Like It*:

> All the world's a stage,
> And all the men and women merely players:
> They have their exits and their entrances;
> And one man in his time plays many parts,
> His acts being seven ages.
>
> (2.7.139-143)

But apart from likening the world at large to the world of the stage, Shakespeare goes further by drawing on the technical language of acting in order to get to the heart of a character's motivation, plight, and intention. Seeing a player become imaginatively overwhelmed during the delivery of a long speech, Hamlet is forced to reflect on his own weak resolve: "What would he do, had he the motive and the cue for passion that I have?" (2.2.561-563). Sometimes the motivational language in Shakespeare is so keen and sharp it verges on contemporary notions of psychological acting, as in these lines of Brutus from *Julius Caesar*:

> Since Cassius did whet me against Caesar,
> I have not slept.
> Between the acting of a dreadful thing
> And the first motion, all the interim is
> Like a phantasma or a hideous dream:
>
> (2.1.61-64)

How these abundant and useful indications of acting filter into Shakespeare's language on a regular basis is partly what learning to act Shakespeare is all about; particularly when an actor encounters a long soliloquy and must work alone. In the form of a script, Shakespeare really gives the actor a score. The beats and units of his speeches are marked with metaphors and images, vocal sounds and stresses, repetitions and interruptions, and pauses and silences. There is a conscious recognition on the playwright's part that actors need these textual "cues" in order to perform words and sentences. The actor who learns to follow Shakespeare's internal direction learns best how to act him. We can begin the process by looking at the smallest of these units, the blank verse line.

The medium of Shakespeare's message and the assortment of acting cues he lays out for the performer are imbedded in the chain of words that make up his speeches. When not written in straightforward prose (which accounts for about 25% of the lines), the plays are most often written in blank verse. Blank verse is nothing more than *unrhyming* verse, interrupted occasionally by rhyming words and couplets. Blank verse is predictable and fairly strict in its rhythmical pattern or meter: five *unstressed* or short sounds (x) alternated or counterpointed for effect by five *stressed* or long sounds (/). The more technical term for this is iambic pentameter, which simply translated means five metrical units of alternating short and long sounds that add up to a total of ten beats:

> x   /   x   /   x   /   x   /   x   /
> di *dum* di *dum* di *dum* di *dum* di *dum*

In regular blank verse the stress is always placed on the second sound, with the whole iambic pentameter line ending in a strong (/) stress regardless of punctuation:

```
                        x   /  x   /  x  / x   / x   /
(HAMLET)                Be thou as chaste as ice, as pure as snow

                        x   /  x   /  x   /  x   / x   /
(RICHARD III)           A horse! A horse! My kingdom for a horse!

                        x  / x  / x   / x   /  x   /
(DUKE ORSINO)           If music be the food of love, play on,
```

Blank verse gives the actor's speech a vocal musicality. It also makes verse sound closer to natural speech, and even today we often speak in blank verse without noticing it. It provides the performer with an efficient means of delivery and an effective tool for remembering long passages, solely through the device of repetitious rhythms. And, together with punctuation, it allows the actor wide latitude in the choice of the stress and color given certain words and phrases. Each of the above lines looks metrically the same. But the *intention* of each one is very different and alters even further when spoken by individual actors. Blank verse guides the actor without shackling his or her delivery or performance. It keeps the performer on track within the score of words, but allows him or her to endlessly invent new possibilities with the words themselves. It does not limit but, in fact, frees the performer to add emphasis to his or her role.

More often than not, Shakespeare will break the potentially singsong and monotonous cadence of regular blank verse by placing added stresses in off-beat positions:

```
                   /   /  x x  x    /   /   /   /   /
(HENRY V)   Once more unto the breach, dear friends, once more

                  x  / x  / x  /  / x x   /  x
(HAMLET)   To be or not to be, that is the question
```

The added strong stresses in these lines from *Henry V* and *Hamlet* introduce a variety for the speaker that also underscores his dramatic intention. King Henry is urging his troops on in an assault over the sounds of battle and alarums. He must be heard above the clamor. Hamlet, who ends his line with an unstressed *eleventh* syllable (called a *feminine ending*) is pointing up a distinction between *being* and *non-being*. He strains to be as precise as possible about an abstract thought and wants the audience to take special note of it. In scanning Shakespeare's speeches for stresses, the actor enters a world of varied expressive shadings. And Shakespeare focuses the stresses to give him or her the freedom to explore the unlimited reaches of an intention.

When you look more carefully at the stressed and unstressed parts of a Shakespearean line, you become aware of the fact that Shakespeare has imbedded a subtext for the actor in the *stressed* words that clearly charts a direction that his or her acting intention might follow, often in very concrete ways. Notice how these stressed words from all the lines above indicate the characters' intentions and obsessions:

> *thou chaste ice pure snow*
> *horse horse king for horse*
> *mus*(ic) *be food love on*
> *Once more breach dear friends once more*
> *be not be that* (is) *quest*

You begin to see that Shakespeare has planted deliberate intentions for the actor that are unmistakably private bits of direction. This kind of notated shorthand, within the larger unit of a whole line, allows the actor to uncover something vital in his character. The alert actor will pick up the cues and see even more clearly what a character is really saying and doing. These hidden notes urge an actor on more specifically than the whole line might seem to be doing in a general way.

Such intentional patterns demonstrate that Shakespeare was not aimlessly writing attractive words and phrases but *loading* the words with directions for an actor's use. The meaning of the words is not so much the issue here as is the impulse they give to a performer. It is this self-directional and intentional quality in all of Shakespeare's language that help give his speeches their playable results.

Let's go further by looking at a two-line interchange from *Henry IV, Part 2*. It will take us deeper into the heart of the matter of acting Shakespeare. The lines are from the famous moment when Prince Hal, now crowned King Henry V, rejects and renunciates his old comic companion Sir John Falstaff. Falstaff begins by greeting the young King on a crowded public street near Westminster Abbey. Cathedral bells might be heard in the distance as he speaks:

	x / x / x / x / x /
(FALSTAFF)	My *king*! My *Jove*! I *speak* to *thee* my *heart*!

	x / x / / / / x x /
(KING HENRY)	I *know* thee *not, old man. Fall* to thy *prayers*.

Notice immediately that Falstaff's line is in perfectly measured iambic pentameter: ten alternating stresses, grouped in four phrases separated by punctuation, and ending with a strong and telling stress on *heart*. Look at how the line colors and ornaments Falstaff's affections for Hal: abundant, elegiac, resounding, and romantic. Falstaff's line is a celebratory one; a statement of both homage and kinship. Its strong monosyllables and intentional pattern *(king Jove speak thee heart)* give the verse line a ringing quality, almost as if "fat" Jack Falstaff were one of the Westminster cathedral bells, tolling at the coronation of the new King. With a classical allusion to the god Jove, he places Hal on an Olympian plane, elevating and separating him from everyone else in the scene. The intentional stresses magnify all that is rich, generous, and fulsome in Falstaff's character. Hearing the words spoken with their exclamation points, we see that Shakespeare directs the actor to *declare* the lines in salute. We also remember that the *Henry* plays have been martial dramas, focused on soldiers and fighting. So Falstaff is also like a huge cannon firing triumphant volleys.

We can even imagine that the clamor of bells and Falstaff's words are followed by a long pause, so that the air can clear and become silent from the ringing echoes. The line is replete with the crackle of consonants: k's, j's, s's, h's, and t's. These, too, help to characterize Falstaff and affect his delivery. Some of these same consonants make up his name. With a full stop at the end of the line, the momentary pause prepares the way for Hal's reply. And it is here that the acting variety of blank verse takes a turn.

Notice, first of all, that Hal's line is *irregular*. In the way that I have scanned the line above, it is disrupted by offbeat stresses on *old* and *fall*. Rather than musically measured clusters, the King's speech is separated into two periodic units. They stress finality and, perhaps, harsh anger. *Know* and *not* sound negative. They are declarative and menacing sentences. The variety built into the off-stressed sounds suggests that an individual actor can give further readings with wholly different stresses as in the three examples on the next page.

```
  /  x     x  /  /  /    /  x  /    x
  I  know thee not, old man. Fall to thy prayers.
```

```
   /  /     x  /  /  /    /  x x      x
   I know thee not, old man. Fall to thy prayers.
```

```
  /  /   /  /  /  /    /  /  /    /
  I know thee not, old man. Fall to thy prayers.
```

In each case the tension and threat build in Hal's lines. They dramatize him. The intentional variations only accent and reinforce his role as a ruler speaking to an underling. His intention is to stop Falstaff in his tracks, and then to put him down, literally, on his knees in servitude and homage. The standing of the two characters is no longer equal. Master lords above servant. He even says he does not know Falstaff. Now very close to the end of the play, this is a climactic turning point in a relationship that has been building in complexity over the course of the two parts of *Henry IV*. After Henry finishes the rest of his speech, he will never look upon Falstaff again. In acting terms, the line is a major change and revelation for Hal's character. No longer a boisterous Prince who loved the company of carousing and familiar companions like Falstaff, Hal assumes the role of the more responsible and sober "King Henry." In this one line of verse, he firmly establishes a new character, forgetting his former self, and points us to the next play in the trilogy, *Henry V*. In order to assume his grip on majesty, Henry must cut Falstaff down to size and put him in his proper place. Falstaff is now merely an ordinary subject and no longer a boon companion.

Like Falstaff, the King uses monosyllables to parallel the appearance of Falstaff's line. The effect, however, is remarkably different. Falstaff's words reach upwards,

Henry's downwards. The King stresses vowels rather than consonants: i's, o's, e's, and a's. The rounded vocality in the o's, especially, caricature the rotundity of Falstaff. Henry's words do not ring, they pound, beating Falstaff down to his knees. The very word *Fall* is a deliberate pun on Falstaff's name as well as a command. As in all of Shakespeare's verse, the richness of sounds has a physical impact. Henry practically bludgeons Falstaff with his phrases.

We can notice even more in this simple but rich line. Through the mere pause between a comma and period, Hal isolates the phrase *old man*, both characterizing Falstaff and demeaning him in public. Falstaff's vigor and strength are deflated in this *old man*, an old man being quite distant from the *Jove*-like King. Hal's lines begin a spectacle of public humiliation, with the peers of the realm onstage and the theatre audiences as witnesses of Henry's new-found power. Henry's sentences are, indeed, a kind of "sentencing" and expulsion of Falstaff from the King's favor. Falstaff's warmth, familiarity, and openheartedness are contradicted and made antithetical by Henry's cold and banishing rebuke. These are icy sentences, frosty in their withering directness and candor. Happy Jack is sliced down to size and deflated by Hard Harry.

The irregularity in blank verse gives an actor sudden mobility and freedom. The actor playing Hal has all kinds of possible choices to aid him in his aggressive attack on Falstaff. He can deliver Hal's lines as dismissively, offhandedly, or dictatorially as he wishes. But the very structure and makeup of Shakespeare's sentences cue the actor to a specific range of intentions: ending and severing a very special kind of relationship. It is up to the actors to make that intention clear through their individual means of expression.

In this brief example, you can see both the economy and variety that Shakespeare builds into his intentional cues. And when he pits the *regularity* against the *irregularity* of his verse lines, the rich antitheses that result explode in a tense and dramatic moment. Only the acting of this exchange and not the mere reading of it can expose its theatrical impact.

The actor should take the entire structure of Shakespeare's lines very seriously. Although modern editors of his plays approach the texts differently, changing marks of punctuation and even words that differ in Quarto and Folio editions of the plays, we have arrived at some basic notions about Shakespeare's sentences. The actor does himself and herself a favor by obeying the punctuation in the speeches. Half-lines usually mean that a pause is called for; a moment is there to ponder. Here is an example from Macbeth's speech after hearing of Lady Macbeth's death:

> Life's but a walking shadow, a poor player
> That struts and frets his hour upon the stage,
> And then is heard no more. It is a tale
> Told by an idiot, full of sound and fury,
> Signifying nothing. [Here is the half-line.]
>   *(Enter a Messenger)*
> Thou com'st to use thy tongue; thy story quickly!

The half-line gives the actor time to register the emptiness of the word "nothing" before quickly responding to the Messenger.

Monosyllables and polysyllables have different weights and values. The opening Chorus speech in *Henry V*, "O for a Muse of fire," is bright and quick. But Macbeth's "Tomorrow, and tomorrow, and tomorrow" is slow and ponderous, like a dull clock ticking away the seconds of a life. But Hamlet's "O that this too, too solid flesh," although largely monosyllabic, is equally ponderous. Juliet's "Gallop apace you fiery-footed steeds" has polysyllables, but races. The actor must give the words their due recognition in the act of performing them. There are no easy and simple rules to follow except obeying Shakespeare's sound score. What you begin to notice is that Shakespeare traffics his words through their vocal colors. And he gives you paths and by-ways that lead you through a speech until you begin to act him with your own kind of courage and authority.

The Shakespeare Monologues

Soliloquies and set speeches have a pride of place in both Shakespeare's plays and those of other Elizabethan and Jacobean playwrights. The origin of the soliloquy lies in classical sources, particularly the Latin plays, poems, and orations that Shakespeare would have probably learned by heart as a schoolboy. Its roots also lie in the highly rhetorical medieval dramas that influenced the evolution of English Renaissance plays. Elizabethan society itself, with its formalities, proclamations, love of liturgy, song, poetry, and majesty was, by its nature, a world in which the soliloquy found a comfortable place. Shakespeare's society was a world of language. His vocabulary alone numbers over 30,000 words, many of them newly invented by him or others. Rarely has language undergone such an expansion as it did during the age of Shakespeare.

The true soliloquy is a speech that an actor delivers alone onstage, either to himself/herself or the audience. Its format is a convention because no actor can speak in isolation. There must be a listener, an audience. So, really, the soliloquy is always meant to be overheard by the audience. Very often in Shakespeare long speeches, or monologues, are delivered by characters to other players onstage. In both cases there is a listener, a crucial fact which must never be forgotten.

Shakespeare's monologues take many different guises. And all the speeches in this book fall into one or more of these categories: interior monologues, pitiful laments, romantic outpourings, angry harangues, confessions and asides, comic wordplays, expository and didactic lectures, rhetorical declamations, and solemn resolutions centering on death. The infinite variety of Shakespeare's monologues makes it difficult to lock them into precise categories. Often several types of monologues appear in one. Usually in the "Commentary" following each of the speeches, we have tried to tell the actor the exact kind of speech he or she is performing. Each one has its own moods and conventions, its own kind of language.

Acting a speech *solus*, alone onstage, was common in Shakespeare's day. The very notion of the Elizabethan platform stage, thrust out into the center of the audience with listeners all around it, served the actor to the audience on a plate. John Heywood, writing in 1612 in his *Apology for Actors*, graphically highlights the solo actor and his roots as orator:

> Whatsoever is commendable in the grave Orator, is most exquisitley perfect in him; for by a full and significant action of body, he charmes our attention: sit in a full Theater, and you will thinke you see so many lines drawne from the circumference of so many eares, whiles the *Actor* is the *Center*.

Heywood may have been describing Shakespeare's favorite actor, Richard Burbage, the best solo actor of his day. In *Hamlet*, Burbage was given a speech by Shakespeare that best sums up what every actor ought to know and often forgets. All great actors of Shakespeare point to this speech, again and again, as the best single source of advice for playing Shakespeare. It is also one of the best

prose monologues in the plays. Here is the first part where
the lesson plan is laid out:

HAMLET
    Speak the speech, I pray you, as I pronounced it to
    you, trippingly on the tongue. But if you mouth it,
    as many of your players do, I had as lief the town
    crier spoke my lines. Nor do not saw the air too
5 much with your hand, thus, but use all gently; for
    in the very torrent, tempest, and as I may say the
    whirlwind of your passion, you must acquire and
    beget a temperance that may give it smoothness.
    O, it offends me to the soul to hear a robustious,
10 periwig-pated fellow tear a passion to tatters, to
    very rags, to split the ears of the groundlings, who
    for the most part are capable of nothing but inex-
    plicable dumb shows and noise. I would have such
    a fellow whipped for o'erdoing Termagant. It out-
15 Herods Herod. Pray you avoid it. Be not too tame,
    neither. But let your own discretion be your tutor.
    Suit the action to the word, the word to the action,
    with this special observance: that you o'erstep not
    the modesty of nature. For anything so overdone is
20 from the purpose of playing, whose end, both at
    the first and now, was and is, to hold, as 'twere,
    the mirror up to nature, to show virtue her own
    feature, scorn her own image, and the very age
    and body of the time his form and pressure . . . .

(3.2.1-25)

In this monologue the actor can begin to see how
Shakespeare's language works as one word and idea build
to tell a story through narration. Although written in
prose, notice how the patterns of the words resemble the
rhythm of blank verse. Words play with and off each other
in unison and opposition. Good and bad acting compete
for attention. The good always comes away sounding
grand and sincere, and the bad atrociously false and
farcical.

Look at the emphasis Hamlet gives to certain words: "speak," "speech," "pronounced," "tongue," "mouth," "crier," and "spoke." But rather than being a lesson in elocution, Hamlet urges the actor to emphasize the *manner* in which he or she performs them so that the *matter* will come shining through. He asks the actor to focus on his instrument—body and voice—and on the best means of delivering a playwright's *intention*. Above all else, the actor's craft should strive for "temperance," "smoothness," the balance of "action" to "word" and "word" to "action." Naturalness must always temper the histrionic and stylized quality inherent in any drama. The actor, in fact, is our mirror. His acts and words are our very reflection.

Hamlet's speech is like a director giving "notes" to an actor before he or she goes onstage to perform. And that is precisely the dramatic situation at this point. The speech is casual and colloquial, even though the pattern of words is formally crafted. It breaks down any barriers between the speaker and listeners. It draws us in and takes us along as any speech from the stage should.

This second soliloquy is something altogether different. The unnatural Richard of Gloucester (later the murderous Richard III) is about as far removed from the natural Prince of Denmark as any character can be. He is, in fact, more like the Devil, the Prince of Darkness. And Richard is very much meant to be the personification of the character Vice from the medieval morality plays. He is cut from the same cloth as Iago and Macbeth. But what he shares with Hamlet, and so many other of Shakespeare's men and women, is a love of the stage and an audience. It is almost impossible to get him off it. He dominates the play from start to finish and is rarely absent for a moment. When the play opens, we see him already rooted to the stage as though he had been born on that very spot just seconds before. He beckons us into the center of his thoughts:

RICHARD OF GLOUCESTER
    Now is the winter of our discontent
    Made glorious summer by this son of York;
    And all the clouds that loured upon our house
    In the deep bosom of the ocean buried.
5   Now are our brows bound with victorious wreaths,
    Our bruisèd arms hung up for monuments,
    Our stern alarums changed to merry meetings,
    Our dreadful marches to delightful measures.
    Grim-visaged war hath smoothed his wrinkled front,
10 And now—instead of mounting barbèd steeds
    To fright the souls of fearful adversaries—
    He capers nimbly in a lady's bedchamber
    To the lascivious pleasing of a lute.
    But I, that am not shaped for sportive tricks
15 Nor made to court an amorous looking glass;
    I, that am rudely stamped, and want love's majesty
    To strut before a wanton ambling nymph;
    I, that am curtailed of this fair proportion,
    Cheated of feature by dissembling Nature,
20 Deformed, unfinished, sent before my time
    Into this breathing world scarce half made up—
    And that so lamely and unfashionable
    That dogs bark at me as I halt by them—
    Why, I, in this weak piping time of peace
25 Have no delight to pass away the time,
    Unless to spy my shadow in the sun
    And descant on my own deformity.
    And therefore, since I cannot prove a lover
    To entertain these fair well-spoken days,
30 I am determined to prove a villain
    And hate the idle pleasures of these days.
    Plots have I laid, inductions dangerous,
    By drunken prophecies, libels and dreams,
    To set my brother Clarence and the King
35 In deadly hate the one against the other.
    And if King Edward be as true and just
    As I am subtle, false, and treacherous,
    This day should Clarence closely be mewed up
    About a prophecy that says that "G"
40 Of Edward's heirs the murderer shall be.

Apart from his formal Prologues, this is the only instance where Shakespeare allows a central character to begin a play with a soliloquy. He experiments here with a
dominant character beside whom all other players in the
action are mere props. Richard, ugly and deformed, is a
master with language. It is his major and only attraction.
And here he woos us, the audience, just as he will later,
outrageously, woo Lady Anne to be his wife.

Even a quick glossing of this speech, in formal blank
verse, shows the excitement of acting Richard. He is una-
bashedly theatrical. His openly stressed *"Now,"* repeated
twice more in the opening section of the speech, shoots out
at the audience, commanding our attention. It immediately
brings us into the action. His irregular verse lines are full
of mean wit and antitheses: "winter"/"summer"; "discon-
tent"/"glorious." There is an instant pun on "son"/"sun"
that pays off later on when Richard talks about spying his
"shadow in the sun." The rising and falling of lines 4-5
("clouds" to "ocean buried"), climbs up again to "victorious
wreaths" and "hung up for monuments" in lines 5-6. Then
two more antitheses: "stern alarums"/"merry meetings";
"dreadful marches"/"delightful measures." The balances
within the sentences show what a controlling speaker Richard is. The images dance together in harmony even though
opposed. War is personified (lines 9-13) as a lascivious lord
and lecher, profaning the very idea of a gracious lord and
courtier. The entire speech is in three parts (lines 1-13; 14-27;
28-41), this being only the first section. Most of Shakespeare's soliloquies follow this three-part structure, giving
the actor the task of working on smaller "speeches" within
a total unit. The speech becomes a small play of its own.

In the second part of the speech, right after he Prologue-like has set the stage for us (wartime turned to
peacetime), Richard becomes uncomfortably familiar with

us, switching to the personal "I." Notice how the measured phrases of the opening section suddenly give way to a catalog of Richard's deformities; all in one long sentence! The semicolons along the way let the actor rest and regain breath through the twisting narrows of Richard's serpentine thoughts. Here we understand why the character is so often portrayed as a viperous reptile. His language literally snakes across the page with its hissing consonants. He also alludes here to the actor's cosmetic art ("made up") and that "mirror" image ("looking glass") that Hamlet used so effectively in his speech. The lively action of dogs *barking* accents the fact that verbs are dominant here. The whole section ends with the polysyllabic vowels in "deformity"; a word that has a chilling echo.

Having stripped himself bare, Richard takes us into his confidence by telling us his secret plots to become King. This is where the solo actor must really work hard for a result. So insidious is Richard, he literally intends to implicate *us* in his crimes. We become part of his conspiracy because we have the knowledge (the "dramatic irony") that other characters lack. The actor, throughout the speech, feigns familiarity with us in order to *win* us over. Richard's art is the actor's art. He is a melodramatic villain to be sure, constantly in danger of "out-Heroding Herod." But he must touch us and take us along with him so that we do not betray him to others. As much as Hamlet, Richard is a master of soliloquies like this one. Through them he displays all the different vocabularies of the actor's craft. And as with any monologue, *persuasion* is the final intention.

Shakespeare's women are not given nearly the number or variety of speeches as his men. Female roles were not played by women but by boys. All accounts suggest that these boy actors were extremely good performers. We also know, from Japanese Kabuki theatre, that men in women's roles can be uncommonly effective.

Although women are not given the broad range of the men's roles, they do have a depth of emotion and, particularly, *vision* that repeats in monologue after monologue. The very limited constraints that a woman in Shakespeare's society faced—daughter, wife, mistress, mother, queen, bawd, witch, madwoman—shows the progression of his female characters. Somewhere on this spectrum each of his women finds her role. Sometimes she has a dominant part in the action, like Cleopatra or Queen Margaret; elsewhere she is subservient and a victim, like Ophelia or Desdemona. They are best when they are partners with men in the drama, like Lady Macbeth. And they excel as characters in the romantic and comic plays: Rosalind, Viola, Beatrice, Juliet, Miranda, Helena, Portia, Cressida, etc. Here is where Shakespeare's women almost eclipse the men. It is certainly in these plays that some of the best speeches are found.

To use a brief example, here is a speech by Miranda from *The Tempest*. It comes very early in the action soon after the storm has destroyed a ship at sea. Miranda speaks to her father, who may be standing somewhere above her:

MIRANDA

    If by your art, my dearest father, you have
    Put the wild oceans in this roar, allay them.
    The sky, it seems, would pour down stinking pitch
    But that the sea, mounting to the welkin's cheek,
5   Dashes the fire out. O, I have suffered
    With those that I saw suffer! A brave vessel—
    Who had no doubt some noble creatures in her—
    Dashed all to pieces! O, the cry did knock
    Against my very heart! Poor souls, they perished!
    Had I been any god of power, I would
10 Have sunk the sea within the earth or ere
    It should the good ship so have swallowed and
    The fraughting souls within her.

It is common to all of Shakespeare's women that their seer-like vision is their strongest asset. It makes up for their lack of physical strength and power. Miranda's speech, like the more famous one by Portia in *The Merchant of Venice*, is about the quality of mercy. She pleads with her father above the final roars of a storm. The lines stress her subservient position to her father, but her rich emotions free an independent life of character. Miranda is suffering because she has *seen* suffering. Without challenging her father directly (it was Prospero who caused the storm that sank the ship), she recaptures the horror of the event which creates it own kind of indictment. She has lived on this island, which she and Prospero inhabit, for most of her life, becoming a creature of nature. Fire, water, air, and earth find their way into her speech, releasing, for the actress, powers that parallel the magical strengths of her father. The speech and its words capture the sense of drowning. Miranda steps into the role as victim and helpless savior.

In a way, Miranda is the essential Shakespearean heroine. She is innocent, a daughter, eventually a lover and wife, a waif, potentially a witch, and, in moments like this, assertive. She expresses the best parts of Shakespeare's women. Her youth makes her seem like a young actress at the start of her career. Shakespeare gives her but a short speech. But the powerful potential in the words and its assertive "I" show that the intention for the actor is to grip and shake the emotions of the lines. From a bright example like this, a glint though it is, the actor sees what brilliant lights Shakespeare has in store for her in other great monologues.

Notes from the Editors

Our brief "introduction" to each speech gives the actor certain cues that will help launch him or her into the dramatic situation. Sometimes we have left in specific "cue lines" to provide more context to ignite the actor. The speeches are followed by "glossary notes" that explain difficult words and passages or highlight something the actor might want to notice in particular. The "Commentaries" try to sample some of the riches in the monologues from an acting point of view. They *do not* tell the performer "how to act" a speech, but are rather appreciations of Shakespeare's skill and ingenuity. These brief comments are merely one person's observations, and the reader is very free to argue or contradict what is said in the "Commentaries."

In the "Selected Bibliography," we refer you to some of the best of the more recent and available work written about acting Shakespeare. The literature on this topic is woefully slight, however. And probably the best "textbook" remains Shakespeare's infinite capacity to challenge and test the actor's talents through his plays.

Any reader or actor must realize that reading an isolated speech outside its rightful dramatic place smacks of artificiality. Shakespeare's lines must always be returned to the plays as quickly as possible. Yet looking at the speeches in isolation duplicates the condition of the Elizabethan actor who was given only his "part" of the play to work on alone, often without the benefit of a rehearsal with other actors. So working in isolation on a Shakespeare speech is how it all began and continues to begin for the actor.

The sampling of speeches here is but a slight gleaning

of a rich harvest. There are well over 500 such speeches in Shakespeare. If *Soliloquy!* does anything, it should challenge you, the actor, to discover Shakespeare again and again on your own.

Michael Earley
Philippa Keil

* * *

These volumes are dedicated to the fond memory of Bernard Beckerman. Our gracious thanks to our publisher Glenn Young for his support and patience during the work on these books.

ALL'S WELL THAT ENDS WELL

Helena

*Act 1, Scene 1. Rousillon (France). The Count's palace.
Helena, daughter of a famous physician, now dead, and
ward of the dowager Countess, loves the young Count
Bertram who is indifferent to her. He has just left for
the court of the King of France. Helena speaks of her
passion and Bertram's high position.*

HELENA
                              I think not on my father,°
     And these great tears grace his° remembrance more
80   Than those I shed for him. What was he° like?
     I have forgot him. My imagination
     Carries no favor° in't but Bertram's.
     I am undone.° There is no living, none,
     If Bertram be away. 'Twere all one
85   That° I should love a bright particular star
     And think to wed it, he is so above me.°
     In his bright radiance and collateral° light
     Must I be comforted, not in his sphere.°
     Th'ambition° in my love thus plagues itself.
90   The hind° that would be mated by the lion
     Must die for love. 'Twas pretty, though a plague,°
     To see him every hour, to sit and draw
     His archèd brows, his hawking° eye, his curls
     In our heart's table°—heart° too capable°
95   Of every line and trick° of his sweet favor.
     But now he's gone, and my idolatrous fancy°
     Must sanctify his relics.° Who comes here?
     (Enter Parolles)
     One that goes with him.° I love him for his sake°—
     And yet I know him a notorious liar,
100 Think him a great way° fool, solely a coward.

1

Yet these fixed° evils sit so fit in him
That they take place° when virtue's steely bones
Looks bleak i'th' cold wind. Withal, full oft° we see
Cold wisdom waiting on° superfluous folly.

78 **father**/(Physician to the old Count and both now dead, his low position has made Helena a gentlewoman by birth. As an orphan, Helena is left to make her own way in the world.) 79 **his**/(she may be referring to Bertram here rather than her father) 80 **he**/i.e., her father 82 **favor**/face 83 **undone**/ruined (also a sexual meaning, *seduced*) 84-85 'Twere...That/it is just as if 86 **above me**/i.e., in nobility and indifference 87 **collateral**/indirect, shining from a different sphere 87-88 **In...sphere**/i.e., he is in an orbit different from hers and shines with a stronger light 89 **ambition**/lofty aims 90 **hind**/female deer or servant 91 **plague**/torment 93 **hawking**/piercing 94 **table**/drawing board **heart**/(pun on *hart* or stag, with the allusion to *hind* above) **capable**/susceptible 95 **trick**/trait 96 **fancy**/love 97 **relics**/that which serves as a memory 98 **One...him**/(Parolles is a friend of Bertram's and is going with him to visit the King's court.) **sake**/advantage 100 **a great way**/largely a 101 **fixed**/firm 102 **take place**/find 103 **Withal, full oft**/Besides, frequently 104 **waiting on**/serving

Commentary: Helena's romantic soliloquy shows her two sides: passionate idolatry for Bertram and, with the entry of Parolles, a cunning knowingness that sees through fools. She can be imploring, but also ruthless. Later in a scene set in Italy, she will manipulate her way into Bertram's bed, doing whatever it takes to win the cool and unloving young Count. Helena is unique among Shakespeare's heroines in her plots to advance to a higher station in life. Note how she instantly forgets her father's memory in order to bring the image of Bertram to the fore of her imagination (lines 78-82). Having firmly fixed him there, wedding him compels each of her motivations and intentions. Her love is an "ambition." And her picture of him is firmly etched (lines 92-95). The pining rhetoric of her verse suddenly gives way to a calculated measurement of the cowardly braggart Parolles (line 99). The irony of the speech is that Helena is blinded by love's tears. She cannot take the full measure of Bertram's foolishness. But her single-minded pursuit of him wins him in the end.

ALL'S WELL THAT ENDS WELL

Helena

Act 1, Scene 3. Rousillon. The Count's palace. Helena, ward to the dowager Countess, is pushed into openly declaring her love for the Countess's son Bertram. The Countess has learned that Helena intends to steal off to Paris in pursuit of her love.

[COUNTESS
    Do you love my son?
HELENA   Your pardon, noble mistress.
COUNTESS
    Love you my son?
HELENA   Do not you love him, madam?
COUNTESS
    Go not about. My love hath in't a bond
185 Whereof the world takes note. Come, come, disclose
    The state of your affection, for your passions
    Have to the full appeached.°]
HELENA   Then I confess,
    Here on my knee, before high heaven and you,
    That before you and next unto high heaven
190 I love your son.
    My friends° were poor but honest;° so's my love.
    Be not offended, for it hurts not him
    That he is loved of° me. I follow him not
    By any token of presumptuous suit,°
195 Nor would I have him till I do deserve him,
    Yet never know how that desert° should be.
    I know I love in vain, strive against hope;
    Yet in this captious° and intenible sieve°
    I still pour in the waters of my love
200 And lack not to lose still.° Thus, Indian-like,°
    Religious in mine error, I adore

3

The sun° that looks upon his worshipper
But knows of him no more. My dearest madam,
Let not your hate encounter° with my love
205 For loving where you do; but if yourself,
Whose agèd honor cites° a virtuous youth,
Did ever in so true a flame° of liking°
Wish chastely and love dearly, that your Dian°
Was both herself and Love,° O then give pity
210 To her whose state° is such that cannot choose
But lend and give where she is sure to lose,
That seeks to find not that her search implies,°
But riddle-like° lives sweetly where she dies.

187 **appeached**/accused 191 **friends**/family, relatives **honest**/honorable
193 **of**/by 194 **token...suit**/sign of presumed wooing 196 **desert**/action
meriting reward 198 **captious**/confusing, entangling **intenible sieve**/
receptacle incapable of holding love 200 **lack...still**/i.e., so overflowing a
love that the surplus is poured away **Indian-like**/i.e., North American
Indian native 202 **sun**/i.e., Bertram, who is likened to the pagan sun god of
Indians 204 **encounter**/oppose 206 **cites**/testifies to (legal word) 207
flame/passion **liking**/loving 208 **Dian**/Diana, goddess of chastity and
virtue 209 **Love**/Venus, goddess of love and passion 210 **state**/emotional
condition and social position 212 **implies**/involves 213 **riddle-like**/
paradoxically

Commentary: Helena's romantic monologue is in the form of a
defense speech. Up to the point of her confession (line 187-190),
Helena's answers have come hard upon the Countess's prosecutorial
questions. Together they mate into single lines of formal regular
verse. The long pause at the half-line (190) gives space for the actor
to recover from her blatant confession and devise a strategy to woo
the Countess to her position. Helena, though ward of the Countess,
is a low gentlewoman by birth and now an orphan. Her declaration
of love for the young Count is a brazen admission, especially since
she places her love for Bertram "before" her love for the Countess
(to whom she owes deep affection and gratitude) and just behind her
love for heaven. Continuing the formality of her declaration,
Helena personalizes her plea by asking the Countess (at line 205) to
place herself in the same position. It is a good strategy, because the
Countess had earlier remarked how like in passion and ardor she
was to Helena in her own youth. Helena's lines are marked by their
strong honesty and sincerity. She is a prisoner of love, kneeling in
suit to a motherly confessor.

ALL'S WELL THAT ENDS WELL

Helena

Act 3, Scene 2. Rousillon. The Count's palace. The young Count Bertram has been forced to marry the lowborn gentlewoman Helena. But shunning her, he has gone to fight a war in Italy. He sends a letter to Helena, saying that he will never return to France until their marriage is dissolved. Helena suffers fatal grief at the news. She plans suicide.

HELENA "Till I have no wife I have nothing in
    France."
  Nothing in France until he has no wife!
  Thou shalt have none, Rousillon,° none in France;
  Then hast thou all again. Poor lord, is't I
105 That chase thee from thy country and expose
  Those tender limbs of thine to the event°
  Of the none-sparing° war? And is it I
  That drive thee from the sportive° court, where
    thou
  Wast shot at with fair eyes, to be the mark°
110 Of smoky muskets? O you leaden messengers°
  That ride upon the violent speed of fire,
  Fly with false aim, cleave the still-piecing° air
  That sings° with piercing, do not touch my lord.
  Whoever shoots at him, I set him there.°
115 Whoever charges on his forward breast,
  I am the caitiff° that do hold° him to't,
  And though I kill him not, I am the cause
  His death was so effected.° Better 'twere
  I met the ravin° lion when he roared
120 With sharp constraint of hunger; better 'twere
  That all the miseries which nature owes°

Were mine at once. No, come thou home,
    Rousillon,
Whence honor but of danger wins a scar,
As oft it loses all.° I will be gone;
125 My being here it is that holds thee hence.
Shall I stay here to do't?° No, no, although
The air of paradise did fan the house
And angels officed° all. I will be gone,
That pitiful rumor may report my flight
130 To consolate thine ear. Come night, end day!
For with the dark, poor thief, I'll steal away.

103 **Rousillon**/i.e., Bertram, Count of Rousillon 106 **event**/outcome, consequence 107 **none-sparing**/in which none are spared 108 **sportive**/ entertaining 109 **mark**/target 110 **leaden messengers**/bullets 112 **still-piecing**/i.e., always closing up and repairing itself 113 **sings**/i.e., whistles with the sounds of bullets 114 **I...there**/(Helena takes responsibility for sending Bertram to Italy) 116 **caitiff**/wretch **hold**/force 117-118 **And though...effected**/i.e., Even if I don't kill him myself, I will have been the reason for his death no matter how he dies 119 **ravin**/ravenous 121 **owes**/ owns 123-124**Whence...all**/i.e., from danger the best that can be won is a scar, but more often death 126 **Shall...to do it?**/Shall I commit suicide? (The verse line is shortened here, suggesting that Helena stops to ponder this point.) 128 **officed**/served

Commentary: Helena's soliloquy is a lament. The letter she received from Bertram read: "When thou canst get the ring upon my finger which shall never come off, and show me a child begotten of thy body that I am father to, then call me husband; but in such a 'then', I write a 'never'." Helena grieves for herself, but more for the danger that Bertram will be exposed to in war, especially the bullets. She feels she has driven him into danger. The verse lines are stricken with bitter reproaches that open the way for suicidal thoughts. Normally a cunning and resourceful woman, Helena is totally at the mercy of her passion for Bertram. He comes before her, not only because of his high position, but because of the enslavement she feels towards him. Fearing the worst that can happen to Bertram—death—Helena's intention is to put herself in an equally fatal position and flee the court to her own kind of exile. Later, she will make her way to Italy and, through a plot, win Bertram according to the terms of the above letter, getting his ring and his child.

6

ANTONY AND CLEOPATRA

Cleopatra

*Act 1, Scene 5. Alexandria. Cleopatra's palace. Political
unrest and the death of his wife Fulvia have made
Antony, Cleopatra's lover, return to Rome from Egypt.
Oppressed by boredom, Cleopatra yearns for him and
sends him daily love letters. She speaks to her maid
Charmian.*

CLEOPATRA   O, Charmian,
    Where think'st thou he is now? Stands he or sits
      he?
20   Or does he walk? Or is he on his horse?°
    O happy horse, to bear the weight of Antony!
    Do bravely,° horse, for wot'st thou° whom thou
      mov'st?—
    The demi-Atlas° of this earth, the arm
    And burgonet° of men. He's speaking now,
25   Or murmuring° "Where's my serpent of old
      Nile?"—
    For so he calls me. Now I feed° myself
    With most delicious poison. Think on me,
    That am with Phoebus'° amorous pinches black,°
    And wrinkled deep in time. Broad-fronted Caesar,°
30   When thou wast here above the ground I was
    A morsel for a monarch, and great Pompey°
    Would stand and make his eyes grow in my brow.
    There would he anchor his aspect,° and die°
    With looking on his life.

20 **horse**/(sexual meaning: to *mount* a woman as though she were a horse)
22 **bravely**/excellently   **wot'st thou**/do you know   23 **Atlas**/supported the
world on his shoulders (*demi* because he shares power with Octavius
Caesar)   24 **burgonet**/helmet   25 **murmuring**/i.e., like a lover   26 **feed**/i.e.,
drinks the drug mixture of mandragola   28 **Phoebus**/Roman sun god
black/i.e., deeply tanned by the sun and wrinkled (also amorous pun on

being pinched black and blue) 29 **Caesar**/Julius Caesar, a former lover, long before Antony 31 **Pompey**/son of Pompey the great, another former lover 33 **aspect**/gaze 33 **die**/die and live at the same time (also sexual meaning with "anchor," i.e., *orgasm*)

Commentary: Cleopatra began this scene by asking her maid Charmian for the drug mandragola—a narcotic plant—so that she "might sleep out this great gap of time/My Antony is away." The Antony that is in her thoughts is an active, amorous lover, and so her words have a provocative meaning: "O happy horse, to bear the weight of Antony!" The effect of the verse is to give absent Antony a real presence and voice in the scene: "'Where's my serpent of Old Nile?'" So Cleopatra gives him body, weight and things to say. The speech also hints at Cleopatra's age. Although she would have been played by a boy actor, she is most often today played by a mature actress. Lines like "serpent of Old Nile" and "wrinkled deep in time" give credibility to that interpretation. She has already had long affairs with Julius Caesar and then Pompey. The historical Cleopatra was 28 when she met Antony and 39 when she died. Yet she also speaks with the flirtatiousness of a teenager in the flush of first romance. See how rushed her questions are until line 23. Her instantaneous shifts from girl to woman are a constant in the play.

ANTONY AND CLEOPATRA

Cleopatra

Act 4, Scene 15. Alexandria. Cleopatra's monument.
Cleopatra has just fainted at the death of her lover,
Antony. Her attendants revive her, calling "Lady,"
"Madame," "Royal Egypt" and "Empress."

CLEOPATRA (*recovering*)
    No more but e'en a woman,° and commanded
    By such poor passion as the maid that milks
75 And does the meanest chores. It were° for me
    To throw my sceptre at the injurious gods,
    To tell them that this world did equal theirs
    Till they had stol'n our jewel.° All's but naught.°
    Patience is sottish,° and impatience does
80 Become a dog that's mad. Then is it sin
    To rush into the secret house of death
    Ere death dare come to us?° How do° you, women?
    What, what, good cheer! Why, how now,
        Charmian?
    My noble girls! Ah, women, women! Look,
85 Our lamp is spent, it's out. Good sirs,° take heart;
    We'll bury him, and then what's brave, what's
        noble,
    Let's do it after the high Roman fashion,
    And make death proud to take us. Come, away.
    This case° of that huge spirit now is cold.
90 Ah, women, women! Come. We have no friend
    But resolution, and the briefest end.
       (*Exeunt, those above bearing off Antony's body*)

---

73 **e'en a woman**/just a woman (and not a queen) 75 **were**/would be
fitting 78 **jewel**/i.e., Antony (also sexual meaning, *chastity*) **naught**/
worthless, wicked (*naughty*) 79 **sottish**/stupid 80-82 **Then...us**/

9

(contemplating suicide) **do**/are 85 **sirs**/(used as a form of address equally to women as men) 89 **case**/body

Commentary: Cleopatra's more thoughtful speeches come in the midst of active scenes like this, where something climactic has just happened. In fact, Cleopatra never has a full soliloquy, alone, in the play. She always seems to be playing to an audience (usually men or her attendants), even at moments of heightened grief. Notice how her speech is not about Antony at all, but about what kind of *show* to put on for "death." The actor needs to examine and question just how real is her passion for Antony? When he *upstages* her with his suicide, she faints, but then immediately recovers. A lot of play-acting is called for in her part. Her death scene will be a grand affair. The tangible body of Antony is both the lifeless "case" of a dead lover and a sort of stage prop. And Cleopatra can make a great deal out of nothing and loss. Note the spectacle that ends the speech.

ANTONY AND CLEOPATRA

Cleopatra

Act 5, Scene 2. Alexandria. Cleopatra's monument.
Octavius Caesar, fearing that Cleopatra will kill herself
over Antony's death and spoil the pleasure of
capturing her alive, sends a guard to watch over her.
Here she tells one of the guards, Dolabella, about her
dream of Antony in which he appears like a legendary
god.

CLEOPATRA
    No matter, sir, what I have heard or known.
    You laugh when boys or women tell their dreams;
75 Is't not your trick?°
[DOLABELLA   I understand not, madam.]
CLEOPATRA
    I dreamt there was an Emperor Antony.
    O, such another sleep, that I might see
    But such another man!
[DOLABELLA   If it might please ye—]
CLEOPATRA
    His face was as the heav'ns, and therein stuck
80 A sun and moon, which kept their course and
       lighted
    The little O o'th' earth.°
[DOLABELLA   Most sovereign creature—]
CLEOPATRA
    His legs bestrid° the ocean; his reared° arm
    Crested the world. His voice was propertied°
    As all the tunèd spheres,° and that to friends;
85 But when he meant to quail° and shake the orb,°
    He was as rattling thunder. For his bounty,°
    There was no winter° in't; an autumn 'twas,
    That grew the more by reaping. His delights

11

Were dolphin-like;° they showed his back above
90   The element they lived in. In his livery°
Walked crowns and crownets.° Realms and islands
were
As plates° dropped from his pocket.
[DOLABELLA   Cleopatra—]
CLEOPATRA
Think you there was, or might be, such a man
As this I dreamt of?

75 trick/habit (also *sexual strategem*) 81 **The little...earth**/The little globe
("O") of the earth (The meaning is not totally clear. This may be a theatrical
pun on the *wooden O* of the Globe Theatre. But one cannot also dismiss
the fact that this is also a very seductive sentence. Much of the speech can
be delivered in a provocative manner for the sake of Dolabella.) 82
bestrid/straddled **reared**/raised 83 **propertied**/possessed of qualities
84 **tunèd spheres**/harmony of the planets 85 **quail**/overpower **orb**/globe
86 **bounty**/generosity 87 **winter**/coldness 89 **dolphin-like**/leaping and
playful 90 **livery**/service 91 **crowns and crownets**/kings and princes 92
plates/silver coins

Commentary: In this speech Cleopatra memorializes Antony's
greatness. Up to this point, it has never been certain just how deeply
she cares for Antony. But once she starts eulogizing him, there is no
stopping her. Dolabella can only make an effort to vainly get in a
few words. His stiff and awkward presence suits Cleopatra's
purpose, because she can use him as a base measure of noble Antony.
Cleopatra is so given to highly-strung and hyperbolic metaphors
that it really doesn't matter if Antony was any of the things she
says he was. He probably was not. It is Cleopatra's nature to wax
lyrical and invest her lovers with a presence and qualities she
imagines they have. Her verse is quick and nimble. Proof of this is
Dolabella's being unable to find a pause long enough to complete a
whole sentence. And Cleopatra plays his clumsiness for all it is
worth. She literally weaves a speech around him like a seductive
serpent. Note the heavy use of sibilants ("S" sounds) that can, when
consciously stressed, have a hypnotic quality. Also note her
conscious use of the "O" sound.

ANTONY AND CLEOPATRA

Cleopatra

Act 5, Scene 2. Alexandria. Cleopatra's monument. Left briefly alone by the Roman guards, Cleopatra prepares to commit suicide and to join her dead lover Antony in Cyndus where they first met. She will go in her best attire. Poisonous asps have been smuggled into her chamber in a basket of figs.

(Enter Iras with a robe, crown, and other jewels)
CLEOPATRA
280 Give me my robe. Put on my crown. I have
    Immortal longings° in me. Now no more
    The juice° of Egypt's grape shall moist this lip.
    (Charmian and Iras help her to dress)
    Yare,° yare, good Iras, quick—methinks I hear
    Antony call: I see him rouse° himself
285 To praise my noble act. I hear him mock
    The luck of Caesar, which the gods give men
    To excuse their after wrath. Husband, I come.
    Now to that name my courage prove my title.°
    I am fire and air; my other elements
290 I give to baser life.° So, have you done?°
    Come then, and take the last warmth of my lips.
    (She kisses them)
    Farewell, kind Charmian. Iras, long farewell.
    (Iras falls and dies)
    Have I the aspic° in my lips? Dost fall?
    If thou and nature can so gently part,
295 The stroke of death is as a lover's pinch,
    Which hurts and is desired. Dost thou lie still?
    If thus thou vanishest, thou tell'st the world
    It is not worth leave-taking.°

281 **Immortal longings**/variety of meanings: longings for death or afterlife; goddess-like desires; or even sexual wordplay on *immoral longings* (Cleopatra's speech is so full of double entendres, they give second meanings to everything she says.) 282 **juice**/wine 283 **Yare**/quickly (ship's command) 284 **rouse**/stir, awaken (also sexual pun on *arousal*) 288 **title**/right 289-290 **I am...life**/i.e., man was believed composed of four elements: fire and air (spiritual sides), earth and water (mortal sides) 290 **done**/i.e., finished dressing her 293 **aspic**/poison of the asp 298 **leave-taking**/taking leave of

Commentary: Throughout the first part of this monologue Cleopatra is being robed in cloak and crown. She appears like exotic statuary to fit her own apt description of herself moments earlier: "now from head to foot/I am marble constant." Cleopatra prepares for death the way some people prepare for parties. Nowhere else— apart from Enobarbus' great description of her and her barge at Cyndus—is the theatrical nature of Cleopatra more lavishly on display. Antony figures in the speech (lines 283-285) as audience to her "act." Her love of sensual imagery—here centered around the lips—can elevate a deadly intention into an erotic encounter. Even as she dies, Cleopatra chooses to make it a major performance. Death, like "a lover's pinch," is "desired." It is a consummation devoutly wished for.   Whether played broadly or specifically, Cleopatra's death scene always has dramatic impact. It is one long, embroidered exit speech and fond farewell from start to finish.

AS YOU LIKE IT

Rosalind

Act 3, Scene 5.   The Forest of Arden.   Rosalind, disguised as a young man, comes upon two bickering rustics, the shepherdess Phebe and the love-sick shepherd Silvius.   She lectures them both on the proper conduct of true lovers.

ROSALIND *(coming forward)*

35   And why, I pray you? Who might be your mother,
     That you insult, exult, and all at once,°
     Over the wretched? What though you have no
          beauty—
     As, by my faith, I see no more in you
     Than without candle may go dark to bed°—
40   Must you be therefore proud and pitiless?
     Why, what means this? Why do you look on me?°
     I see no more in you than in the ordinary
     Of nature's sale-work.°—'Od's° my little life,
     I think she means to tangle° my eyes, too!
45   No, faith, proud mistress, hope not after it.
     'Tis not your inky brows, your black silk hair,
     Your bugle° eyeballs, nor your cheek of cream,
     That can entame° my spirits to your worship.
     (To Silvius) You, foolish shepherd, wherefore do
          you follow her
50   Like foggy south,° puffing with wind and rain?
     You are a thousand times a properer man
     Than she a woman. 'Tis such fools as you
     That makes the world full of ill-favored children.
     'Tis not her glass° but you that flatters her,
55   And out of you she sees herself more proper
     Than any of her lineaments° can show her.

(To Phebe) But, mistress, know yourself; down on
  your knees
And thank heaven, fasting, for a good man's love;
For I must tell you friendly° in your ear,
60 Sell when you can. You are not for all markets.
Cry the man mercy,° love him, take his offer;
Foul° is most foul, being foul to be a scoffer.—
So, take her to thee, shepherd. Fare you well.

36 **all at once**/i.e., in the same breath 38-39 **As...bed**/i.e., there is nothing particularly fair about you that wouldn't be missed in the dark 41 **Why... me?**/(Phebe is giving Rosalind loving looks) 43 **sale-work**/ready-made goods of indistinct quality **'Od's**/God save us (an oath) 44 **tangle**/ensnare (comes as an aside) 47 **bugle**/decorative, black, glass beads 48 **entame**/subdue 50 **south**/south wind 54 **glass**/mirror 56 **lineaments**/features 59 **friendly**/as a friend 61 **Cry..mercy**/ask the man's forgiveness 63 **Foul**/ugliness, harshness

Commentary: Wounded by love's arrows herself, it is easy for Rosalind (dressed and speaking as the male Ganymede) to take pity on the spurned Silvius and speak harshly to Phebe. Although this is a didactic monologue, calculated to change Phebe's attitude, it has another effect. Phebe switches her affections to the stern Ganymede/Rosalind! The comedy in the scene comes from the mistake in identity. Rosalind, in keeping with her disguise, adopts a "tough guy"/"cool guy" approach in talking to both lovers, switching from one to the other. Her speech lets us know how fetching Phebe is (lines 43-48) and how spineless Silvius is (lines 49-52). Refereeing between the two, Rosalind falls into a little plot complication of her own making as Phebe begins to pursue her/him. You can hear the false male bravado sounded in Rosalind's straightforward use of verse. She/he seems to run out of steam by the end of the speech, bringing lines 62-63 to a kind of chugging halt.

AS YOU LIKE IT

Phebe

Act 3, Scene 5.   Forest of Arden.   Having just been rebuked by Rosalind, dressed as the male youth Ganymede, the saucy shepherdess Phebe becomes infatuated with her/him.   She speaks of the youth to the shepherd Silvius.

PHEBE

Think not I love him, though I ask for him.
110 'Tis but a peevish boy. Yet he talks well.
But what care I for words? Yet words do well
When he that speaks them pleases those that hear.
It is a pretty° youth—not very pretty—
But sure he's proud; and yet his pride becomes
    him.
115 He'll make a proper man. The best thing in him
Is his complexion; and faster than his tongue
Did make offence, his eye did heal it up.
He is not very tall; yet for his years he's tall.
His leg is but so-so; and yet 'tis well.
120 There was a pretty redness in his lip,
A little riper and more lusty-red
Than that mixed in his cheek. 'Twas just the
    difference
Betwixt the constant° red and mingled damask.°
There be some women, Silvius, had they marked
    him
125 In parcels° as I did, would have gone near
To fall in love with him; but for my part,
I love him not, nor hate him not. And yet
Have I more cause to hate him than to love him.
For what had he to do to chide at me?
130 He said mine eyes were black, and my hair black;

17

And now I am remembered,° scorned at me.
I marvel why I answered not again.
But that's all one. Omittance is no quittance.°
I'll write to him a very taunting letter,
135 And thou shalt bear it. Wilt thou, Silvius?

113 **Pretty**/attractive (unintentional reference to the fact that "Ganymede" is a woman) 123 **constant**/uniform **mingled damask**/pink; mixture of white and red 125 **In parcels**/piece by piece 131 **remembered**/reminded 133 **Omittance is no quittance**/i.e., my failure to reply does not mean I won't reply

Commentary: The delight of Phebe's monologue lies in the fact that she unwittingly discovers that the youth Ganymede is the maid Rosalind. Ironically, Phebe translates each of Rosalind's female qualities into attractive male ones. She dwells on "his" complexion, eyes, lips, and stature. The speech echoes the mistaken identities that cause the plot complications in the play at large. Phebe is not a seminal character in the action, and this is really her only juicy scene in the whole play.

AS YOU LIKE IT

Rosalind

Epilogue. The stage. Rosalind delivers this speech to the audience after the actors have left the stage. It is really her only soliloquy in the play of any length.

ROSALIND *(to the audience)* It is not the fashion to see
the lady the epilogue; but it is no more
unhandsome° than to see the lord the prologue. If
it be true that good wine needs no bush,° 'tis true
5 that a good play needs no epilogue. Yet to good
wine they do use good bushes, and good plays
prove the better by the help of good epilogues.
What a case° am I in then, that am neither a good
epilogue nor cannot insinuate° with you in the
10 behalf of a good play! I am not furnished° like a
beggar, therefore to beg will not become me. My
way is to conjure° you; and I'll begin with the
women. I charge you, O women, for the love you
bear to men, to like as much of this play as please
15 you. And I charge you, O men, for the love you
bear to women—as I perceive by your simpering°
none of you hates them—that between you and the
women the play may please. If I were a woman° I
would kiss as many of you as had beards that
20 pleased me, complexions that liked me, and breaths
that I defied° not. And I am sure, as many as have
good beards, or good faces, or sweet breaths will for
my kind offer, when I make curtsy, bid me
farewell.°

3 **unhandsome**/unbecoming   4 **no bush**/no advertisement (i.e., the
vintner's bush)   8 **case**/predicament (Also reference to "her" *encasement*
in male costume.)   9 **insinuate**/ingratiate   10 **furnished**/dressed   12
conjure/charm   16 **simpering**/coy smiles (Smiling, perhaps, in the

19

knowledge that this "woman" speaking to them is a boy actor.)   18
If...woman/(ironic comment on the fact of being a boy)   21 **defied**/disliked
23-24 **bid me farewell**/i.e., applaud me

Commentary: The chief intention of the epilogue is to offer a last
bit of entertainment. The actor is in some twilight role mid-way
between the character and himself. Normally epilogues allowed
the actor to show-off some theatrical feat, dancing or singing. Here
the effect seems to be dexterity with words. For the speech is full of
wit and wordplays. The moralizing tone is very soft. The prose is
not particularly striking. But it does have a sweetness and honesty
that has characterized so much of Rosalind throughout the action.
The speech plays on the intentional multiple irony of a boy (actor)
playing a girl (character) playing a boy in disguise playing the
Epilogue (boy actor). Notice how "she" toys with the men and the
women in the speech to reinforce the point.

THE COMEDY OF ERRORS

Adriana

Act 2, Scene 2. Ephesus. The marketplace. Adriana, the much abused and confused wife of Antipholus of Ephesus, encounters his twin brother, Antipholus of Syracuse, in the streets. She entreats him to treat her more kindly, not knowing he is the wrong man.

ADRIANA

Ay, ay, Antipholus, look strange° and frown:
Some other mistress hath thy sweet aspects.°
115 I am not Adriana, nor thy wife.
The time was once when thou unurged wouldst
    vow
That never words were music to thine ear,
That never object pleasing in thine eye,
That never touch well welcome to thy hand,
120 That never meat sweet-savored in thy taste,
Unless I spake, or looked, or touched, or carved to
    thee.°
How comes it now, my husband, O how comes it
That thou art then estrangèd° from thyself?—
Thy "self" I call it, being strange to me
125 That, undividable, incorporate,
Am better than thy dear self's better part.
Ah, do not tear away thyself from me;
For know, my love, as easy mayst thou fall°
A drop of water in the breaking gulf,
130 And take unmingled thence that drop again
Without addition or diminishing,
As take from me thyself, and not me too.
How dearly° would it touch thee to the quick
Shouldst thou but hear I were licentious,°
135 And that this body, consecrate to thee,

By ruffian lust should be contaminate?
Wouldst thou not spit at me, and spurn at me,
And hurl the name of husband in my face,
And tear the stained° skin off my harlot brow,
140 And from my false hand cut the wedding ring,
And break it with a deep-divorcing vow?
I know thou canst, and therefore see thou do it!
I am possessed with an adulterate blot;
My blood is mingled with the crime of lust;
145 For if we two be one, and thou play false,
I do digest the poison of thy flesh,
Being strumpeted by thy contagion.°
Keep then fair league° and truce with thy true bed,
I live unstained, thou undishonorèd.

113 **strange**/unfriendly 114 **aspects**/looks 121 **Unless...thee**/(she collects all the verbs from the previous sentences in this line) 123 **estranged**/alien (one of the main words in the play) 128 **fall**/let fall 133 **dearly**/grievously 134 **licentious**/adulterous 139 **stained**/disfigured 147 **contagion**/ catching disease 148 **league**/alliance

Commentary: Adriana's monologue is full of honest declarations of needs and love. It is also an indirect commentary on divided and unified personality; a theme that two sets of twin brothers makes even more dramatic. This is Shakespeare's earliest comedy, and so none of the characters in *Comedy of Errors* is particularly deep. The play is a farce, and its characters merely need to display single comic traits. But Adriana's speech strikes a level of feeling that usually stands out in any production of the play. The second half of the speech (from line 133) has an unusual power and wrath. Notice the strong verbs. She is a wronged woman ripe for vengeance. And were not the play a farce, she might take strong action. The comic irony is that she is speaking to the wrong Antipholus, so her pleas fall on uncomprehending ears. But in farce genuine feelings are always usurped by some such device.

CORIOLANUS

Volumnia

Act 5, Scene 3. Outside the gates of Rome. Coriolanus'
tent inside the Volscian camp. Laying seige to Rome,
the vengeful Coriolanus has denied each entreaty sent
from the Romans. Finally, his mother comes with his
wife and son to persuade him to retreat.

[CORIOLANUS
    Aufidius and you Volsces, mark, for we'll
    Hear naught from Rome in private.
    (He sits)

                              Your request?]
VOLUMNIA
    Should we be silent and not speak, our raiment
95 And state of bodies would bewray° what life
    We have led since thy exile. Think with thyself
    How more unfortunate than all living women
    Are we come hither, since that thy sight, which
      should
    Make our eyes flow with joy, hearts dance with
      comforts,
100 Constrains them weep and shake with fear and
      sorrow,
    Making the mother, wife, and child, to see
    The son, the husband, and the father tearing
    His country's bowels out; and to poor we
    Thine enmity's most capital.° Thou barr'st us
105 Our prayers to the gods, which is a comfort
    That all but we enjoy. For how can we,
    Alas, how can we for our country pray,
    Whereto we are bound, together with thy victory,
    Whereto we are bound? Alack, or° we must lose
110 The country, our dear nurse, or else thy person,

Our comfort in the country. We must find°
An evident° calamity, though we had
Our wish which side should win. For either thou
Must as a foreign recreant° be led
115 With manacles through our streets, or else
Triumphantly tread on thy country's ruin,
And bear the palm° for having bravely shed
Thy wife and children's blood. For myself, son,
I purpose not to wait on fortune till
120 These wars determine.° If I cannot persuade thee
Rather to show a noble grace° to both parts°
Than seek the end of one, thou shalt no sooner
March to assault thy country than to tread—
Trust to't, thou shalt not—on thy mother's womb
125 That brought thee to this world.

95 **bewray**/reveal 104 **capital**/deadly 109 **or**/either 111 **find**/experience
112 **evident**/certain 114 **recreant**/traitor 117 **palm**/prize of victory 120
determine/come to an end 121 **grace**/indulgence **parts**/parties, sides

Commentary: Volumnia is just as arrogant and willful as her son
Coriolanus. In fact, she is the one person he fears and will be ruled
by. She is fiercely patriotic; possibly more maternal towards Rome
than towards her own son. His assaulting Rome is likened to
treading "on thy mother's womb." Volumnia's verse is full of such
awful imagery. Above, she speaks of Coriolanus "tearing/His
country's bowels out." In anger she can be wrathful and furious. At
one point in the action she says, "Anger's my meat; I sup upon
myself." She presents herself as a kind of barrier. If Coriolanus and
the Volscians are to enter Rome, it will literally be over her dead
body. Whatever sentiment Coriolanus retains (for mother, wife,
child), Volumnia will prey on it (lines 100-104). These are the keys
which will unlock the door of Coriolanus' pity. Note how she lumps
all together in her use of "we." Each victory for Coriolanus is an
antithetical defeat for his family.

CORIOLANUS

Volumnia

*Act 5, Scene 3. Outside the gates of Rome. Coriolanus'
tent inside the Volscian camp. Volumnia continues
her appeal to her son, Coriolanus, to spare Rome.*

[CORIOLANUS
    Not of a woman's tenderness to be
130 Requires nor child nor woman's face to see.
    I have sat too long.
    (He rises and turns away)]
VOLUMNIA   Nay, go not from us thus.
    If it were so that our request did tend
    To save the Romans, thereby to destroy
    The Volsces whom you serve, you might condemn us
135 As poisonous of your honor. No, our suit
    Is that you reconcile them: while the Volsces
    May say "This mercy we have showed," the
        Romans
    "This we received," and each in either side
    Give the all-hail to thee and cry "Be blest
140 For making up this peace!" Thou know'st, great
        son,
    The end of war's uncertain; but this certain,
    That if thou conquer Rome, the benefit
    Which thou shalt thereby reap is such a name
    Whose repetition will be dogged with curses,
145 Whose chronicle° thus writ: "The man was noble,
    But with his last attempt° he wiped it° out,
    Destroyed his country, and his name remains
    To th' ensuing age abhorred." Speak to me, son.
    Thou has affected° the fine strains of honor,
150 To imitate the graces° of the gods,
    To tear with thunder the wide cheeks o'th' air,

And yet to charge thy sulphur° with a bolt
That should but rive° an oak. Why dost not speak?
Think'st thou it honorable for a noble man
155 Still to remember wrongs? Daughter, speak you,
He cares not for your weeping. Speak thou, boy.
Perhaps thy childishness will move him more
Than can our reasons. There's no man in the
  world
More bound to's mother, yet here he lets me prate
160 Like one i'th' stocks.° Thou hast never in thy life
Showed thy dear mother any courtesy,
When she, poor hen, fond of no second brood,
Has clucked thee to the wars and safely home,
Loaden° with honor. Say my request's unjust,
165 And spurn me back. But if it be not so,
Thou art not honest, and the gods will plague thee
That thou restrain'st° from me the duty which
To a mother's part belongs.—He turns away.
Down, ladies. Let us shame him with our knees.
170 To his surname "Coriolanus" 'longs° more pride
Than pity to our prayers. Down! An end.
This is the last.
(The ladies and Young Martius kneel)

145 **chronicle**/history 146 **attempt**/enterprise **it**/nobility 149 **affected**/
aspired to 150 **graces**/mercy 152 **charge thy sulphur**/load thy lightning
153 **rive**/split 160 **stocks**/wooden shackles that confine the legs 164
Loaden/laden 167 **restrain'st**/hold 170 **'longs**/belongs

Commentary: Volumnia's appeal shows her unique skills as a
politician. She presents Coriolanus with options that will allow
him an honorable way out, appeasing the two warring sides (lines
135-140). Confused and unable to speak, Coriolanus' reaction is
difficult to read. So Volumnia presses forward like a mother
prodding a petulant young son. Given the seriousness of what's at
stake in this scene—Rome and survival—Volumnia's speech has an
oddly domestic feel to it. She manages to be huffy and yet controls
the scene. Right after she speaks Coriolanus will surrender to her,
saying, if the gods were to look down on this scene they would

laugh, so unnatural it seems. But Volumnia is the kind of woman who refuses to budge until she gets her way. She uses every motherly trick, even guilt, to this end.

CYMBELINE

Imogen

Act 1, Scene 3. Britain. King Cymbeline's palace. In a rage, the King has banished Posthumus, a poor but worthy gentleman who has secretly married the King's daughter, Imogen.   Here Imogen, locked away in the castle, questions the servant Pisanio about Posthumus' departure by ship.

IMOGEN
> I would have broke mine eye-strings,° cracked
>   them, but
> To look upon him till the diminution
> Of space° had pointed him sharp as my needle;°
> 20 Nay, followed him till he had melted from
> The smallness of a gnat to air, and then
> Have turned mine eye and wept. But, good
>   Pisanio,
> When shall we hear from him?

[PISANIO Be assured, madam,
25 With his next vantage.]

IMOGEN
> I did not take my leave of him, but had
> Most pretty things to say. Ere° I could tell him
> How I would think on him at certain hours,
> Such thoughts and such, or I could make him
>   swear
> 30 The shes° of Italy should not betray
> Mine interest° and his honor, or have charged him
> At the sixth hour of morn, at noon, at midnight
> T'encounter me with orisons°—for then
> I am in heaven for him—or ere I could
> 35 Give him that parting kiss which I had set
> Betwixt two charming° words, comes in my father,

And, like the tyrannous breathing of the north,
Shakes all our buds from growing.

17 **eye-strings**/(it was thought that the eye muscles would snap when
under too great a strain) 19 **space**/distance **needle**/i.e., point of a needle
27 **Ere**/before 30 **shes**/women 31 **interest**/right, claim 33 **T'encounter...
orisons**/i.e., join me in prayers 36 **charming**/spells, protections against
evil

Commentary: Imogen is one of Shakespeare's purest heroines,
noted for her constancy and the beauty of her verse lines. Here she
delivers a lament about not being able to see the departure of her
new husband from Britain's shores. The intensity and physical
strain of looking overwhelms the opening line. Then the words
"eye" and "I" never quite let us forget the power of this vision. The
images in the opening lines—"eye-strings," "needle" and "gnat"—
are so sharp and precise. The foreboding sense of betrayal at line 30
adds an early frost to the speech and, coupled with the final lines,
lets us know that the marriage of the young couple is new and subject
to storm and testing.

CYMBELINE

Imogen

Act 3, Scene 2. Britain. Cymbeline's palace. Leonatus Posthumus sends a letter to his young wife, Imogen, with the false news that he is returning to Britain from Italy. Wrongly believing that Imogen has committed adultery during his absence, he has also sent a letter to his servant Pisanio, ordering him to kill Imogen.

[PISANIO
25   Madam, here is a letter from my lord.
IMOGEN
    Who, thy lord that is my lord, Leonatus?°
    O learned indeed were that astronomer°
    That knew the stars as I his characters°—
    He'd lay the future open.] You good gods,
30   Let what is here contained° relish of love,
    Of my lord's health, of his content—yet not°
    That we two are asunder;° let that grieve him.
    Some griefs are med'cinable;° that is one of them,
    For it doth physic love°—of his content
35   All but in that. Good wax,° thy leave. Blest be
    You bees that make these locks of counsel!° Lovers
    And men in dangerous bonds° pray not alike;
    Though forfeiters° you cast in prison, yet
    You clasp young Cupid's tables.° Good news, gods!
    (She opens and reads the letter)°
40   "Justice and your father's wrath, should he take°
    me in his dominion, could not be so cruel to me as
    you, O the dearest of creatures, would even renew
    me with your eyes. Take notice that I am in
    Cambria,° at Milford Haven. What your own love

45 will out of this advise you, follow. So he wishes
    you all happiness, that remains loyal to his vow,
    and your increasing in love,
                          Leonatus Posthumus."
    O for a horse with wings! Hear'st thou, Pisanio?
    He is at Milford Haven. Read, and tell me
50 How far 'tis thither. If one of mean affairs°
    May plod it in a week, why may not I
    Glide thither in a day? Then, true° Pisanio,
    Who long'st like me to see thy lord, who long'st—
    O let me bate°—but not like me—yet long'st
55 But in a fainter kind—O, not like me!
    For mine's beyond beyond; say, and speak thick°—
    Love's counsellor should fill the bores of hearing,°
    To th' smothering of the sense—how far it is
    To this same blessèd Milford. And by th' way°
60 Tell me how Wales was made so happy as
    T'inherit such a haven. But first of all,
    How we may steal° from hence; and for the gap
    That we shall make in time° from our hence-going
    Till our return, to excuse; but first, how get hence?
65 Why should excuse be born or ere begot?°
    We'll talk of that hereafter. Prithee speak,
    How many score of miles may we well ride
    'Twixt hour and hour?

26 **Who...Leonatus?**/(The intentional lack of clarity in the line shows
Imogen's bursting excitement at the news.) 27 **astronomer**/astrologer 28
characters/handwriting 30 **here contained**/i.e., in the letter 31 **not**/not
content 32 **asunder**/apart 33 **med'cinable**/healing, restorative 34 **physic
love**/keep love healthy 35 **Good wax**/(she refers to the sealing wax on the
letter, which she begins to open) 36 **locks of counsel**/private seals 37
bonds/contracts 38 **forfeiters**/contract violators 39 **Cupid's tables**/i.e.,
Love's letters or notebooks SD/(She might pause for a whole line to take in
the contents of the letter.) 40 **take**/find (Posthumus has been banished
from Britain by King Cymbeline) 44 **Cambria**/Wales 50 **mean affairs**/
unimportant business 52 **true**/faithful (intended irony, since Pisanio has
been ordered to kill Imogen once on the road to Milford Haven) 54
bate/modify 56 **thick**/fully 57 **bores of hearing**/ears 59 **by th' way**/
while you're at it 62 **steal**/sneak off 62-63 **the gap...time**/i.e., the length of
time we will be missing (Note here how quickly Imogen is speaking and

how jammed her sentences are getting.) 65 **Why...begot?**/i.e., why worry
about excuses before the need is conceived

Commentary: Just before delivering this false news to Imogen,
Pisanio has a soliloquy in which he discloses Leonatus' order to kill
Imogen for adulterous acts that have been wrongly reported by a
villain named Iachimo. The tension in the scene comes from
Imogen's excitement and Pisanio's deadly charge (he later decides
she is too virtuous to murder). Imogen's verse is marked by its
anticipation and swiftness. Her enthusiasm is unbridled and her
sentences rush forward; sometimes they contain several thoughts
simultaneously or else jam-up (lines 53-59). She asks Pisanio
questions and doesn't even wait for answers. Her long speculation on
the distance from the palace to the port of Milford Haven—where
Posthumus supposedly waits for her, but where Pisanio is to kill
her—is full of unchecked sentence fragments (lines 48-68). One
imagines that the actor is as physically charged with movement as
are her words. Imogen has the impetuous spirit of Juliet in her.

CYMBELINE

Imogen

Act 3, Scene 6. Wales. Before the cave of Belarius.
Imogen, dressed like a boy, has escaped from her father,
King Cymbeline, and hopes to make her way to Italy
and to her husband Posthumus. But lost in the Welsh
hills, she finds herself before the cave of the banished
nobleman who kidnapped her brothers when infants.

IMOGEN
I see a man's life is a tedious one.
I have tired myself, and for two nights together
Have made the ground my bed. I should be sick,
But that my resolution helps me. Milford,°
5 When from the mountain-top Pisanio showed
    thee,
Thou wast within a ken.° O Jove, I think
Foundations° fly the wretched—such, I mean,
Where they should be relieved. Two beggars told
    me
I could not miss my way. Will poor folks lie,
10 That have afflictions° on them, knowing 'tis
A punishment or trial? Yes. No wonder,
When rich ones scarce tell true. To lapse in
    fullness°
Is sorer° than to lie for need, and falsehood
Is worse in kings than beggars. My dear lord,
15 Thou art one o'th' false ones. Now I think on thee
My hunger's gone, but even° before I was
At point to sink° for food. But what is this?°
Here is a path to't. 'Tis some savage hold.°
I were best not call; I dare not call; yet famine
20 Ere clean° it o'erthrow nature, makes it valiant.
Plenty and peace breeds cowards; hardness° ever

33

Of hardiness is mother. Ho! Who's here?
If anything that's civil,° speak; if savage,
Take or lend.° Ho! No answer? Then I'll enter.
25 Best draw my sword, and if mine enemy
But fear the sword like me, he'll scarcely look on't.
Such° a foe, good heavens!

4 **Milford**/Milford Haven port 6 **a ken**/eyeshot, view 7 **Foundations**/
charity, alms 10 **afflictions**/sufferings 12 **To lapse in fullness**/to lie even
though well off 13 **sorer**/worse 16 **even**/just 17 **At...sink**/about to faint
this/(sees the cave) 18 **savage hold**/animal's den 20 **Ere clean**/before
completely 21 **hardness**/hardship 23 **civil**/civilized 24 **Take or lend**/rob
or give 27 **Such**/i.e., send such

Commentary: Since the play *Cymbeline* is a romance, a fairy
tale, it is only right that Imogen should be directed off course and
lost in the woods for a while. Her soliloquy is about trials that test
and strengthen resolve: "hardness ever/Of hardiness is mother."
Imogen is one of Shakespeare's questing heroines (another is
Rosalind in *As You Like It*), who leave the comforts of the court
behind to strike out in search of love and freedom. "Plenty and
peace breeds cowards," she says. After overcoming a series of tests,
they arrive safely at their goal. The cave behind her offers the
actor a wonderful obstacle to play with: the dark dangerous
unknown. It is a triumph of intention over adversity and fear when
Imogen makes the decision to enter the cave at the close of her
courage-bolstering speech.

CYMBELINE

Imogen

Act 4, Scene 2. Britain. Before the cave of Belarius.
Imogen awakens from a drug-induced sleep to find the
headless body of her pursuer Cloten dressed in the
garments of her husband Posthumus. While she was
asleep, Cloten was killed and beheaded by Imogen's
brother, Guiderius.

IMOGEN (*awakes*)

    Yes, sir, to Milford Haven.° Which is the way?
    I thank you. By yon bush? Pray, how far thither?
    'Od's pitykins,° can it be six mile yet?
    I have gone° all night. 'Faith, I'll lie down and
       sleep.
    (*She sees Cloten*)
295 But soft, no bedfellow! O gods and goddesses!
    These flowers are like the pleasures of the world;
    This bloody man the care on't. I hope I dream,
    For so° I thought I was a cavekeeper,°
    And cook to honest creatures. But 'tis not so.
300 'Twas but a bolt° of nothing, shot of nothing,
    Which the brain makes of fumes.° Our very eyes
    Are sometimes like our judgements, blind. Good
      faith,
    I tremble still with fear; but if there be
    Yet left in heaven as small a drop° of pity
305 As a wren's eye, feared gods, a part of it!
    The dream's here still. Even when I wake it is
    Without me as within me; not imagined, felt.
    A headless man? The garments of Posthumus?
    I know the shape of's leg; this is his hand,
310 His foot Mercurial,° his Martial° thigh,
    The brawns of Hercules; but his Jovial° face—

Murder in heaven! How? 'Tis gone. Pisanio,
All curses madded Hecuba° gave the Greeks,
And mine to boot, be darted° on thee! Thou,
315 Conspired with that irregulous° devil Cloten,
Hath here cut off my lord. To write and read
Be henceforth treacherous! Damned Pisanio
Hath with his forgèd letters—damned Pisanio—
From this most bravest vessel° of the world
320 Struck the main-top!° O Posthumus, alas,
Where is thy head? Where's that? Ay me, where's
that?
Pisanio might have killed thee at the heart
And left thy head on. How should this be?
Pisanio?
'Tis he and Cloten. Malice and lucre° in them
325 Have laid this woe here. O, 'tis pregnant,°
pregnant!
The drug he gave me, which he said was precious
And cordial° to me, have I not found it
Murd'rous to th' senses? That confirms it home.
This is Pisanio's deed, and Cloten—O,
330 Give color to my pale cheek with thy blood,
That we the horrider may seem to those
Which° chance to find us!
(She smears her face with blood)
O my lord, my lord!
(She faints.)

291 **Milford Haven**/i.e., the port that was her destination (Imogen is
drowsy when she awakes, and speaks as if to other travelers she has met
along the way.) 293 **pitykins**/God's little pity 294 **gone**/walked 298 **so**/i.e.,
while dreaming **cavekeeper**/cave dweller 300 **bolt**/shaft 301
fumes/vapors induced by sleep 304 **drop**/tear 310 **Mercurial**/like
Mercury's **Martial**/Mars-like 311 **Jovial**/ Jove-like 313 **Hecuba**/wife of
King Priam of Troy who cursed the slaughtering Greeks 314 **darted**/shot
315 **irregulous**/lawless 319 **bravest vessel**/most handsome body 320
main top/top sail (head) 324 **lucre**/greed 325 **pregnant**/evident 327
cordial/restorative 332 **Which**/who

Commentary: Imogen's soliloquy is about the horror of discovering the dead and mutilated body of a lover (even though the identity is mistaken). The scene is similar to the tomb scene in *Romeo and Juliet.* This is a difficult speech to keep under control because it can so easily lapse into humor, especially line 321: "Where is thy head?"   The whole monologue is charged with melodramatic lamentations and confusions. Note the rhetoric of lines 309-314. But within the excessive moments of the speech we can note some of Imogen's seer-like powers: "but if there be/Yet left in heaven as small a drop of pity/As a wren's eye, feared gods, a part of it!" Yet, the grotesque horror of the moment takes the character closer to madness than to better judgement. This is an instance of theatrical trickery to which the actor must respond histrionically.

HAMLET

Ophelia

Act 2, Scene 1. Elsinore. Polonius' chambers in the castle. Ophelia, terrified and concerned about Hamlet's behavior towards her, confesses his actions to her father.

[OPHELIA
    Alas, my lord, I have been so affrighted.
POLONIUS With what, i'th' name of God?]
OPHELIA
    My lord, as I was sewing in my chamber,°
    Lord Hamlet, with his doublet all unbraced,°
80 No hat upon his head, his stockings fouled,°
    Ungartered, and down-gyvèd° to his ankle,
    Pale° as his shirt, his knees knocking each other,
    And with a look so piteous in purport°
    As if he had been loosèd° out of hell
85 To speak of horrors, he comes before me.
[POLONIUS
    Mad for thy love?
OPHELIA   My lord, I do not know,
    But truly I do fear it.
POLONIUS   What said he?]
OPHELIA
    He took me by the wrist and held me hard,
    Then goes he to the length of all his arm,
90 And with his other hand thus o'er his brow
    He falls to such perusal° of my face
    As a would draw it. Long stayed he so.
    At last, a little shaking of mine arm,
    And thrice his head thus waving up and down,
95 He raised a sigh so piteous and profound°
    That it did seem to shatter all his bulk°

38

And end his being.° That done, he lets me go,
And, with his head over his shoulder turned,
He seemed to find his way without his eyes,
100 For out o'doors he went without their help,
And to the last° bended° their light on me.

78 **chamber**/closet, private room 79 **doublet all unbraced**/jacket all
unlaced 80 **fouled**/filthy 81 **down-gyved**/i.e., hanging down like fetters on
a prisoner's legs 82 **Pale**/white 83 **purport**/meaning 84 **loosed**/released
91 **perusal**/study 95 **profound**/deep 96 **bulk**/body 97 **being**/life 101
last/ end **bended**/aimed

Commentary: Ophelia's monologue is pure exposition. It is a
description of how Hamlet looks and acts. Whether his actions are
real or feigned ("the trappings and suits of woe") is never known;
the important point here is that Ophelia *believes* what she sees.
For Ophelia, her vision of Hamlet is akin to Hamlet's vision of the
ghost. Notice that nothing is said. Her speech gives the Prince an
other-wordly character. The grabbing of her wrist is a sudden
reminder of pain for the actor (line 88), helping her remember all
the finely-etched details that follow (lines 89-99). This is the only
mention in the play of direct physical contact between Hamlet and
Ophelia, and it is a detail that can stimulate motivation.

HAMLET

Ophelia

Act 3, Scene 1.   Elsinore.   Somewhere in the castle.
Hamlet has just cruelly admonished Ophelia for no
apparent reason.   He seems mad and shaken with rage.
Her fear is apparent in what she says.

[HAMLET I have heard of your paintings, too, well
    enough God hath given you one face, and you
    make yourselves another.   You jig, you amble, and
    you lisp, and nickname God's creatures, and make
145 your wantonness your ignorance.   Go to, I'll no
    more on't.   It hath made me mad.   I say we will
    have no more marriages.   Those that are married
    already—all but one—shall live.   The rest shall
    keep as they are.   To a nunnery,° go.   *(Exits)*]
OPHELIA
150 O, what a noble mind is here o'erthrown!
    The courtier's, soldier's, scholar's eye, tongue,
       sword.
    Th'expectancy° and rose° of the fair state,°
    The glass° of fashion and the mold of form,°
    Th'observed° of all observers, quite, quite, down!°
155 And I, of ladies most deject and wretched,
    That sucked the honey of his music° vows,
    Now see that noble and most sovereign° reason
    Like sweet bells jangled out of tune and harsh;
    That unmatched form and feature of blown° youth
160 Blasted° with ecstasy.° O woe is me,
    T'have seen what I have seen, see what I see!

149 **nunnery**/Elizabethan slang for "brothel" 152 **expectancy**/hope **rose**/
ornament, blossom **state**/i.e., Denmark 153 **glass**/mirror **mold of form**/
pattern of courtly behavior 154 **observed**/most watched and noted **down**/
fallen 156 **music**/poetic 157 **sovereign**/ruling 159 **blown**/full blooming
160 **Blasted**/withered **ecstasy**/madness, frenzy

Commentary: Ophelia's soliloquy is the start of her despair and descent into a madness of her own. Throughout the action she has been used as a spy and abused by everyone, appearing to be a character without a mind and will of her own. But her observance of Hamlet is very close and particular; her language has a knowingness that contradicts any claim that she is a vapid, useless pawn. Note her verse phrasing: it is measured and deeply poetic. The last line makes us suddenly aware that Ophelia sees much more deeply than most other characters in the play. Not given many lines to play with, she stands apart and notices what goes on throughout the court. Seeing what she has seen will drive her mad.

HAMLET

Ophelia

Act 4, Scene 5. Elsinore. The castle. The death and secret burial of her father Polonius have driven Ophelia mad. She is allowed to enter Gertrude's presence.

[*Enter Ophelia, mad, her hair down, with a lute*]
OPHELIA
    Where is the beauteous majesty of Denmark?
[QUEEN GERTRUDE How now, Ophelia?]
OPHELIA (*sings*)

        How should I your true love know
        From another one?—
25   By his cockle hat and staff,°
        And his sandal shoon.°

[QUEEN GERTRUDE
    Alas, sweet lady, what imports this song?]
OPHELIA Say you? Nay, pray you, mark.
    (*Sings*)   He° is dead and gone, lady,
30   He is dead and gone.
        At his head a grass-green turf,
        At his heels a stone.
[QUEEN GERTRUDE Nay, but Ophelia—]
OPHELIA Pray you, mark.
    (*Sings*)
35 White his shroud as the mountain snow—
    (*Enter King Claudius*)
[QUEEN GERTRUDE Alas, look here, my lord.]
OPHELIA (*sings*)

        Larded° with sweet flowers,
        Which bewept to the grave did—not—go
        With true-love showers.

[KING CLAUDIUS
40 How do ye, pretty lady?]
OPHELIA Well, God'ield° you. They say the owl was a
    baker's daughter.° Lord, we know what we are, but
    know not what we may be. God be at your table!
[KING CLAUDIUS *(to Gertrude)* Conceit upon her father.]
OPHELIA
45 Pray you, let's have no words of this, but when
    they ask you what it means, say you this
    (Sings)

              Tomorrow is Saint Valentine's day,
                 All in the morning betime,
              And I a maid at your window
50   To be your Valentine.

              Then up he rose, and donned his clothes,
                 And upped the chamber door;
              Let in the maid,° that out a maid
                 Never departed more.

[KING CLAUDIUS
55 Pretty Ophelia—]
OPHELIA Indeed, la? Without an oath, I'll make an
    end on't.
    (Sings)

              By Gis,° and by Saint Charity,
                 Alack, and fie for shame!
              Young men will do't if they come to't,
60   By Cock, they are to blame.
              Quoth she "Before you tumbled me,
                 You promised me to wed."
              So would I 'a' done, by yonder sun,
                 An thou hadst not come to my bed.

[KING CLAUDIUS *(to Gertrude)*
65 How long hath she been thus?]

OPHELIA I hope all will be well. We must be patient.
   But I cannot choose but weep to think they should
   lay him i'th' cold ground. My brother shall know
   of it. And so I thank you for your good counsel.
70 Come, my coach! Good night, ladies, good night,
   sweet ladies, good night, good night.

25 **cockle hat and staff**/(a cockleshell on the hat was a common sign of
pilgrims) 26 **shoon**/shoes 29 **He**/Polonius 37 **Larded**/decorated 41
God'ield/God reward 41-42 **They say...daughter**/(allusion to the tale of
the baker's daughter who denied bread to Christ and was turned into an
owl) 54 **maid**/virgin 57 **Gis**/Jesus 57-64 **By Gis...to my bed**/(all the lines
of the song are full of bawdy allusions)

Commentary: Although Ophelia is not a major presence in the
play, with moments like this she makes unforgettable impressions.
Just before her entrance here a Gentleman prepares us saying: "She
is importuante, indeed distract./Her mood will needs be pitied." In
one sense, Ophelia's mood marks the tension and guilt that has
infected the atmosphere of the court. Her song is a funeral dirge
filled with conceits (fanciful notions) and erotic fantasies. She has
had to hold her silence so long in the play that now she exorcises
her imagination and gives it a strange, full voice. Hamlet's
expulsion from Denmark and Polonius' death are a twin release.
Madness is a kind of independence for Ophelia to say and do as she
pleases. It is interesting to note how both the King and Queen seem
to stand in subservient positions to her. She has full command of the
scene; both her entrance and exit are highly theatrical. She is
completely transformed from her last appearance in the play, and
has been offstage for quite some time. So the effect of her
appearance is startling.

HAMLET

Ophelia

Act 4, Scene 5. Elsinore. The castle. Ophelia has been driven mad with grief over the inadvertant murder of Polonius by Hamlet. Her brother Laertes returns from France and finds her in this state.

[VOICES *(within)* Let her come in.
LAERTES How now, what noise is that?
        (Enter Ophelia as before)
155   O heat dry up my brains! Tears seven times salt
      Burn out the sense and virtue of mine eye!
      By heaven, thy madness shall be paid by weight
      Till our scale turns the beam. O rose of May,
      Dear maid, kind sister, sweet Ophelia!
160   O heavens, is't possible a young maid's wits
      Should be as mortal as an old man's life?
      Nature is fine in love, and where 'tis fine
      It sends some precious instance° of itself
      After the thing it loves.]
OPHELIA *(sings)*
165   They bore him barefaced on the bier,
                    Hey non nony, nony, hey nony,
                    And on his grave rained many a tear—
      Fare you well, my dove.°
[LAERTES
      Hadst thou thy wits and didst persuade revenge,
170   It could not move thus.]
OPHELIA You must sing "Down, a-down," and you,
      "Call him a-down-a." O, how the wheel° becomes
      it! It is the false steward that stole his master's
      daughter.
[LAERTES This nothing's more than matter.°]

OPHELIA
175 There's rosemary, that's for remembrance. Pray,
     love, remember.   And there is pansies; that's for
     thoughts.
[LAERTES
     A document° in madness—thoughts and
         remembrance fitted.]
OPHELIA There's fennel for you, and columbines.
180 There's rue for you, and here's some for me. We
     may call it herb-grace o' Sundays. O, you must
     wear your rue with a difference. There's a daisy. I
     would give you some violets, but they withered all
     when my father died. They say a made a good end.
185 *(Sings)* For bonny sweet Robin is all my joy.
[LAERTES
     Thought and affliction, passion, hell itself
     She turns to favor and to prettiness.]
OPHELIA *(sings)*
                    And will a not come again,
                    And will a not come again?
190   No, no, he is dead,
                        Go to thy death-bed,
                    He never will come again

                    His beard as white as snow,
                    All flaxen was his poll.
195   He is gone, he is gone,
                        And we cast away moan.
                    God 'a' mercy on his soul.
             And of all Christian souls, I pray God. God b'wi' ye.

163 **instance**/proof 168 **dove**/spirit 172 **wheel**/(meaning is uncertain,
although it may refer to wheel of fortune; may also indicate a turning action
for the actor) 174 **matter**/nonsense, stuff 178 **document**/lesson

Commentary: Ophelia last appeared before Gertrude and
Claudius only 80 lines earlier. But in that time she has descended

deeper into madness. Much of the grief in the scene has to be translated through Laertes. Ophelia's movements become more important than her words by this point. In fact, the verses of the songs pound out a steady beat. Or they may command her to turn in circles. In essence, the words are music to which the actor choreographs steps. Each structures a different pattern of movement according to its rhythm. Notice how the speech changes from verse to song to prose to song.

HAMLET

Gertrude

Act 4, Scene 7. Elsinore. The castle. Queen Gertrude reports to Laertes the drowning death of his sister, Ophelia.

[QUEEN GERTRUDE
  One woe doth tread upon another's heel,
  So fast they follow. Your sister's drowned, Laertes.
LAERTES
165 Drowned? O, where?]
QUEEN GERTRUDE
  There is a willow grows aslant° a brook
  That shows his hoar° leaves in the glassy stream.
  Therewith fantastic garlands did she make
  Of crow-flowers, nettles, daisies, and long purples,°
170 That liberal° shepherds give a grosser name,
  But our cold maids do dead men's fingers call
    them.
  There on the pendent° boughs her crownet° weeds
  Clamb'ring° to hang, an envious sliver° broke,
  When down the weedy trophies and herself
175 Fell in the weeping brook. Her clothes spread wide,
  And mermaid-like a while they bore her up;
  Which time she chanted snatches of old tunes,
  As one incapable° of her own distress,
  Or like a creature native and endued°
180 Unto that element. But long it could not be
  Till that her garments, heavy with their drink,
  Pulled the poor wretch from her melodious lay
  To muddy death.

---

166 **aslant**/sideways 167 **hoar**/silver-gray 169 **long purples**/wild orchids
170 **liberal**/gross minded 172 **pendent**/hanging **crownet**/coronet 173
Clamb'ring/climbing **envious sliver**/spiteful branch 178 **incapable**/
unawares 179 **endued**/in harmony

48

Commentary: Gertrude's monologue is a highly embroidered exposition speech. The verse is served by a strong use of vowels, meaning that the actor must carefully and slowly stress her lines in order to best serve the descriptive passages. As much as anyone else at this point in the play, Gertrude's own grief and woe is beginning to show. Gertrude appears to enter into Ophelia's state of mind in order to experience the actual drowning. She captures the falling and unstruggling nature of Ophelia's death, "from her melodius lay/To muddy death." The long half-line at the end leaves room for a silent conclusion to the whole description.

HENRY IV, PART 1

Lady Percy

Act 2, Scene 3. Northumberland. Percy's castle. Lord Percy has decided, after troubled deliberation, to join the rebellion against the King. His wife, Lady Percy, enters to try and calm his cares, but also to discover what he has been plotting.

LADY PERCY

O my good lord, why are you thus alone?
For what offence have I this fortnight° been
A banished woman from my Harry's bed?
40 Tell me, sweet lord, what is't that takes from thee
Thy stomach,° pleasure, and thy golden sleep?
Why dost thou bend thine eyes upon the earth,°
And start so often when thou sitt'st alone?
Why hast thou lost the fresh blood in thy cheeks,
45 And given my treasures and my rights of thee
To thick-eyed musing and cursed° melancholy?
In thy faint slumbers° I by thee have watched,
And heard thee murmur tales of iron wars,
Speak terms of manège° to thy bounding steed,
50 Cry "Courage! To the field!" And thou hast talked
Of sallies and retires,° of trenches, tents,
Of palisadoes,° frontiers,° parapets,
Of basilisks,° of cannon, culverin,°
Of prisoners ransomed, and of soldiers slain,
55 And all the currents° of a heady° fight.
Thy spirit within thee hath been so at war,
And thus hath so bestirred thee in thy sleep,
That beads of sweat have stood upon thy brow
Like bubbles in a late-disturbèd stream;
60 And in thy face strange motions° have appeared,
Such as we see when men restrain their breath

On some great sudden hest.° O, what portents° are
   these?
Some heavy business hath my lord in hand,
And I must know it, else he loves me not.

38 **fortnight**/two weeks 41 **stomach**/appetite 42 **bend**...**earth**/look
downcast 46 **cursed**/peevish 47 **faint slumbers**/light sleeps 49 **manège**/
horse training 51 **sallies and retires**/charges and retreats 52 **palisadoes**/
defenses made with sharp stakes **frontiers**/fortifications 53 **basilisks**/
large brass cannons **culverin**/smallest cannons 55 **currents**/flow **heady**/
violent 60 **motions**/movements 62 **hest**/command **portents**/strange
signs

Commentary: Like Calpurnia and Portia in *Julius Caesar*, Lady
Percy is given a monologue that is an attempt to soothe a troubled
husband. There is genuine affection between the couple. Part of the
intention of the speech is to note for us Harry Percy's consternation.
Kate Percy, like her husband Hotspur, does not stand on ceremony.
She dives right in to find out the trouble, pushing and prodding for
an answer. She has obviously listened with relish to Hotspur's
tales of battle because she uses the terms so familiarly (lines 50-55),
translating her fears and concerns into language he can understand.

HENRY IV, Part 2

Lady Percy

Act 2, Scene 3. Warkworth. Before Northumberland's castle. Lady Percy, Hotspur's widow, pleads with her father-in-law, the Earl of Northumberland, to desert the rebel cause and cease fighting the King.

LADY PERCY
O yet, for God's sake, go not to these wars!
10 The time was, father, that you broke your word
When you were more endeared° to it than now—
When your own Percy, when my heart's dear
    Harry,
Threw many a northward look to see his father
Bring up his powers; but he did long in vain.°
15 Who then persuaded you to stay at home?
There were two honors lost, yours and your son's.
For yours, the god of heaven brighten it!
For his, it stuck upon him as the sun
In the grey vault of heaven, and by his light
20 Did all the chivalry of England move
To do brave acts. He was indeed the glass°
Wherein the noble youth did dress themselves.
He° had no legs that practised not his gait;
And speaking thick,° which nature made his
    blemish,
25 Became the accents of the valiant;
For those that could speak low and tardily°
Would turn their own perfection to abuse
To seem like him. So that in speech, in gait,
In diet, in affections° of delight,°
30 In military rules, humors of blood,°
He was the mark° and glass, copy and book,

That fashioned others. And him—O wondrous
   him!
O miracle of men!—Him did you leave,
Second to none, unseconded° by you,
35 To look upon the hideous god of war
In disadvantage, to abide° a field
Where nothing but the sound of Hotspur's name
Did seem defensible;° so you left him.
Never, O never do his ghost the wrong
40 To hold your honor more precise and nice°
With others than with him. Let them alone.
The Marshal and the Archbishop° are strong.
Had my sweet Harry had but half their numbers.
Today might I, hanging on Hotspur's neck,
45 Have talked of Monmouth's° grave.

11 **endeared**/pledged by bond of blood (he failed to come to Hotspur's
aid) 13-14 **Threw...vain**/i.e., vainly waited for Northumberland to appear
with reinforcements 21 **glass**/mirror 23 **He**/i.e., any man 24 **thick**/quickly
(one reason he was called Hotspur) 26 **tardily**/slowly 29 **affections**/
emotions **delight**/pleasure 30 **humors of blood**/temperament 31 **mark**/
example 34 **unseconded**/unsupported (in battle) 36 **abide**/ remain on
38 **defensible**/capable of making a defense 40 **precise and nice**/strict
and scrupulous 42 **Marshall...Archbishop**/i.e., the other rebels to whom
Northumberland is pledged: Lord Mowbray and Scroop, Archbishop of
York 45 **Monmouth**/Prince Hal who killed Hotspur in battle

Commentary: Since the death of Hotspur (Harry Percy) at the
close of *1 Henry IV*, Lady Kate Percy has only had a marginal role.
But here she is given probably the best female speech in the play.
It is an eloquent, convincing monologue about the wastage of war,
and she uses a memorialized image of her dead husband Harry as
the central motif. Honor is her theme. The love between Kate and
Harry was close and rich, which accounts for the honesty in the
verse. As the widow of a valiant soldier, Kate Percy's intention, at
this point, is to keep his memory vividly alive. She also harbors a
resentment towards Northumberland for not coming to Percy's aid in
a fatal battle. Just as Hotspur was anxious for war, Kate is anxious
for peace. The genuineness of her rebuke carries a chilling sting: "so
you left him." In that simple line (38) is contained all she has been
meaning to say. The motivation for her speech boils down to this.

HENRY IV, Part 2

Mistress Quickly

Act 2, Scene 1. A London street. Mistress Quickly, hostess-owner of the Boar's Head Tavern in Eastcheap, is seeking to have Sir John Falstaff arrested for his huge debt. "He hath eaten me out of house and home," is how she frames the charge. Here she encounters Falstaff.

[SIR JOHN
85 *(to the Hostess)* What is the gross sum that I owe thee?]

MISTRESS QUICKLY Marry, if thou wert an honest man, thyself, and the money too. Thou didst swear to me upon a parcel-gilt goblet,° sit-
90   ting in my Dolphin chamber,° at the round table, by a sea-coal° fire, upon Wednesday in Whee-son° week, when the Prince broke thy head for liking° his father to a singing-man of Windsor— thou didst swear to me then, as I was washing
95   thy wound, to marry me, and make me my lady thy wife. Canst thou deny it? Did not goodwife Keech the butcher's wife come in then, and call me "Gossip° Quickly"—coming in to borrow a mess of vinegar, telling us she had a good dish of
100   prawns,° whereby thou didst desire to eat some, whereby I told thee they were ill for a green wound?° And didst thou not, when she was gone downstairs, desire me to be no more so familiarity with such poor people, saying that ere
105   long they should call me "madam?" And didst thou not kiss me, and bid me fetch thee thirty

shillings? I put thee now to thy book-oath;° deny
it if thou canst.
(She weeps.)

89 **parcel-gilt goblet**/cup gilded partly on the inside 90 **Dolphin
chamber**/private drinking room (Dolphin was a common tavern name in
Shakespeare's London) 91 **sea-coal**/mineral coal brought by sea from
Newcastle 91-92 **Wheeson**/Witsun 93 **liking**/comparing 98
Gossip/common form of address between friends 100 **prawns**/shrimp
101-102 **green wound**/new wound 107 **book-oath**/i.e., oath on a Bible

Commentary: Mistress Quickly's monologue is notable for the
vividness of its prose. It is full of rich, colloquial colors that are
made even brighter by her anger at Falstaff. Lines 87-95 are all one
sentence, which ends with the true motivation for her anger:
Falstaff has falsely promised marriage. The speech is framed as a
domestic quarrel, with fear of reputation a central concern. The
ludicrous idea of Mistress Quickly as "Lady" Quickly just doesn't
scan. But that is the humorous intention. The word "wife"—so
important in the speech—is supported by such words as "wert,"
"Wednesday in Wheeson week," "Windsor," and "washing thy
wound." It is echoed twice more in line 96. The fun of the scene
continues right after this when Falstaff wheedles more money from
her. Mistress Quickly is a character in four of Shakespeare's plays
(both parts of *Henry IV*, *Henry V* and *The Merry Wives of
Windsor*).

HENRY V

Mistress Quickly

*Act 2, Scene 3.   London.   In front of the Boar's Head
Tavern in Eastcheap.   Mistress Quickly, owner-hostess
of the tavern, reports on the death of Falstaff ("the King
hath killed his heart") to her husband Pistol and
Falstaff's other cronies.   This is her only brief
appearance in the play.*

[BARDOLPH Would I were with him, wheresome'er he
    is, either in heaven or in hell.]
HOSTESS Nay, sure he's not in hell. He's in
10   Arthur's bosom,° if ever man went to Arthur's
    bosom. A° made a finer end, and went away an it°
    had been any christom° child. A parted ev'n just°
    between twelve and one, ev'n at the turning o'th'
    tide°—for after I saw him fumble with the sheets,
15   and play with flowers, and smile upon his finger's
    end, I knew there was but one way. For his nose
    was as sharp as a pen, and a babbled of green fields.
    "How now, Sir John?" quoth I. "What, man! Be o'
    good cheer." So a cried out, "God, God, God," three
20   or four times. Now I, to comfort him, bid him a
    should not think of God; I hoped there was no need
    to trouble himself with any such thoughts yet. So a
    bade me lay more clothes on his feet. I put my
    hand into the bed and felt them, and they were as
25   cold as any stone. Then I felt to his knees, and so
    up'ard and up'ard, and all was as cold as any stone.

10 **Arthur's bosom**/(malapropism for *Abraham's bosom*, i.e., heaven) 11
A/He (Note that all her phrasings are full of mistakes.) **an it**/as if he 12
christom/christened **ev'n just**/exactly 13-14 **turning o'th' tide**/(a
popular folk belief that marked the moment of death)

Commentary: Nell Quickly has now married Pistol and is just
called Hostess. But her monologue reveals a deep love for the dear
departed Falstaff.   His last moments before death are vividly
portrayed in her prose. It is a lovely bit of colloquial storytelling.
The actor does this kind of speech best by taking time with what
are essentially all monosyllables. It's best not to rush any of it
because this speech, and the whole scene, is a kind of wake. Words
like "God," "cold" and "stone" have a rounded vocality that gives
the speech an intoning quality. She is tolling the "end" of a life.
The half-line at the end (line 25) leaves a long, silent pause. This
can often be a very moving speech about the loss of a loved one.
Note, too, its simple folk qualities.

HENRY VI, Part 1

Joan la Pucelle

Act 1, Scene 2. France. Battlefield near Orléans. Charles the Dauphin receives an unexpected visitor, the shepherdess Joan (Joan of Arc), who tells him of her vision and charge to help the oppressed French to victory in the seige of Orléans.

JOAN

    Dolphin,° I am by birth a shepherd's daughter,
    My wit° untrained in any kind of art.
    Heaven and our Lady gracious hath it pleased
    To shine on my contemptible estate.°
55 Lo, whilst I waited on my tender lambs,
    And to sun's parching heat displayed my cheeks,
    God's mother° deignèd to appear to me,
    And in a vision, full of majesty,
    Willed me to leave my base° vocation
60 And free my country from calamity.
    Her aid she promised, and assured success.
    In complete glory she revealed herself—
    And whereas I was black and swart° before,
    With those clear rays which she infused on me
65 That beauty am I blest with, which you may see.
    Ask me what question thou canst possible,
    And I will answer unpremeditated.°
    My courage try by combat, if thou dar'st,
    And thou shalt find that I exceed my sex.
70 Resolve° on this: thou shalt be fortunate,
    If thou receive me for thy warlike mate.

51 **Dolphin**/Dauphin (eldest son of the King of France)   52 **wit**/intelligence, knowledge 54 **contemptible estate**/scornful, lowly state 57 **God's mother**/ Virgin Mary   59 **base**/lowly   63 **black and swart**/tanned and harsh-complected 67 **unpremeditated**/honestly 70 **Resolve**/be convinced

58

Commentary: At the start of the play, Joan la Pucelle (*pucelle* means *virgin* in French and is perverted to *puzzle* or *whore* by the English) is a simple, straightforward character. A shepherdess called from the sheepfield to the battlefield, her speech to the Dauphin is down-to-earth and unadorned. Even her vision of the Blessed Virgin seems like nothing out of the ordinary, but just an everyday event. Part of what she says sounds like a marriage proposal. And, indeed, she wants to "mate" with Charles, but for war not for sex. She is, as she says, above her sex where France is concerned. She offers Charles a deal he cannot refuse, under the threatening circumstance.

HENRY VI, Part 1

Joan la Pucelle

Act 3, Scene 3. France. Battlefield near Rouen. Fresh from her victory at Rouen, Joan (Joan of Arc) meets the Duke of Burgundy and wins him back to the French cause. He had been siding with the English.

[CHARLES
40   Speak, Pucelle, and enchant him with thy words.]
JOAN
     Brave Burgundy, undoubted hope of France,
     Stay. Let thy humble handmaid° speak to thee.
[BURGUNDY
     Speak on, but be not over-tedious.]
JOAN
     Look on thy country,° look on fertile France,
45   And see the cities and the towns defaced
     By wasting ruin of the cruel foe.
     As looks the mother on her lowly babe
     When death doth close his tender-dying eyes,
     See, see the pining malady of France;
50   Behold the wounds, the most unnatural wounds,
     Which thou thyself hast given her woeful breast.
     O turn thy edgèd° sword another way,
     Strike those that hurt, and hurt not those that help.
     One drop of blood drawn from thy country's bosom
55   Should grieve thee more than streams of foreign
          gore.°
     Return thee, therefore, with a flood of tears,
     And wash away thy country's stainèd spots.
[BURGUNDY *(aside)*
     Either she hath bewitched me with her words,
     Or nature makes me suddenly relent.]

JOAN

60 Besides, all French and France exclaims on° thee,
    Doubting thy birth° and lawful progeny.
    Who join'st thou with but with a lordly nation
    That will not trust thee but for profit's sake?°
    When Talbot hath set footing once in France
65 And fashioned thee that instrument of ill,
    Who then but English Henry will be lord,
    And thou be thrust out like a fugitive?°
    Call we to mind, and mark but this for proof:
    Was not the Duke of Orléans thy foe?
70 And was he not in England prisoner?
    But when they heard he was thine enemy
    They set him free, without his ransom paid,
    In spite of Burgundy and all his friends.
    See, then, thou fight'st against thy countrymen,
75 And join'st with them° will be thy slaughtermen.
    Come, come, return; return, thou wandering lord,
    Charles and the rest will take thee in their arms.

42 **handmaid**/servant 44 **country**/(Burgundy's domain is that part of
France now scarred with battle)   52 **edged**/sharp and two-edged   55
foreign gore/English blood   60 **exclaims on**/loudly accuses   61
birth/nationality 62-63 **Who...sake?**/(Joan sows the doubt in the Duke
that the English are using him for their profit) 67 **fugitive**/a renegade 75
them/those who

Commentary: Always the shepherdess, Joan calls Burgundy back
into the flock (lines 76-77). Her monologue is in the form of a plea or
suit. A maid from the country, Joan persuades Burgundy by focusing
on France as a living but wounded landscape. Her vivid images are
enough to win over the Duke. But part of her strategy is to flatter
and sow doubt in the Duke by, what is later called, "fair persuasion
mixed with sugared words." What probably convinces the Duke
most is when Joan points out (lines 74-75) that the English will
invariably kill him as a traitor. Throughout 1 *Henry VI*, Joan
begins to understand the art of political persuasion, especially when
simple patriotism falls on deaf ears.

HENRY VI, Part 1

Joan la Pucelle

Act 5, Scene 3. France. Battle of Angiers. The French are losing the fight to the English. Joan (Joan of Arc) desperately summons her powers of witchcraft to call forth avenging spirits. But they desert her.

JOAN

The Regent° conquers, and the Frenchmen fly.
Now help, ye charming spells and periapts,°
And ye choice° spirits that admonish° me
And give me signs of future accidents.°
(Thunder)
5 You speedy helpers, that are substitutes°
Under the lordly monarch of the north,°
Appear, and aid me in this enterprise!
(Enter Fiends)
This speed and quick° appearance argues proof°
Of your accustomed diligence to me.
10 Now, ye familiar spirits that are culled°
Out of the powerful regions under earth,
Help me this once, that France may get the field.°
(They walk and speak not)
O, hold me not with silence overlong!
Where I was wont° to feed you with my blood,
15 I'll lop a member° off and give it you
In earnest° of a further benefit,
So you do condescend to help me now.
(They hang their heads)
No hope to have redress?° My body shall
Pay recompense if you will grant my suit.
(They shake their heads)
20 Cannot my body nor blood-sacrifice
Entreat you to your wonted furtherance?°

Then take my soul—my body, soul, and all—
Before that England give the French the foil.°
(They depart)
See, they forsake° me. Now the time is come
25 That France must vail° her lofty-plumèd crest
And let her head fall into England's lap.
My ancient incantations° are too weak,
And hell too strong for me to buckle with.°
Now, France, thy glory droopeth to the dust.
*(Excursions. The Dukes of Burgundy and York
fight hand to hand. The French fly. Joan la Pucelle
is taken.)*

1 **Regent**/Duke of York 2 **periapts**/amulets 3 **choice**/chosen **admonish**/warn 4 **accidents**/events, catastrophes 5 **substitutes**/agents 6 **lordly monarch of the north**/ruler of evil spirits 8 **quick**/living or hasty **argues proof**/proves 10 **culled**/chosen 12 **get the field**/win the battle 14 **wont**/accustomed 15 **member**/breast 15 **earnest**/payment, as a pledge 18 **redress**/remedy, relief 21 **wonted furtherance**/customary assistance 23 **foil**/defeat 24 **forsake**/spurn 25 **vail**/lower 27 **incantations**/spells 28 **buckle with**/close combat (also a sexual meaning)

Commentary: Joan's speech is a series of incantations and spells that make her appear more like a devil than a saint. Throughout the play, Joan has undergone several transformations, from virgin to politician to villain. Here she even takes on the bawdy character of a whore (lines 18-23). Perhaps because she has lost the power of right as a character, the impotent fiends desert her. The image she projects is that of Brueghel's *Dulle Griet*, a madwoman feeding off the battlefields. She began the play as an innocent, avenging guardian angel and here sides with evil. Note how the verse spirals downwards "to the dust." Her power literally fizzles out.

HENRY VI, Part 2

Eleanor

Act 1, Scene 2. London.   The Duke of Gloucester's house.   Eleanor, Duchess of Gloucester, and rival to the newly crowned Queen Margaret, chastises her husband for his lack of ambition.   As Lord Protector to the King, he stands in line to the crown.

DUCHESS

    Why droops my lord, like over-ripened corn
    Hanging the head at Ceres'° plenteous load?
    Why doth the great Duke Humphrey knit his
       brows,
    As frowning at the favors of the world?
5   Why are thine eyes fixed to the sullen° earth,
    Gazing on that which seems to dim thy sight?
    What seest thou there? King Henry's diadem,°
    Enchased° with all the honors of the world?
    If so, gaze on, and grovel on thy face
10 Until thy head be circled with the same.
    Put forth thy hand, reach at the glorious gold.
    What, is't too short? I'll lengthen it with mine;
    And having both together heaved it up,
    We'll both together lift our heads to heaven
15 And never more abase° our sight so low
    As to vouchsafe one glance unto the ground.

2 **Ceres**/goddess of the harvest 5 **sullen**/dull 7 **diadem**/crown 8 **Enchased**/adorned 15 **abase**/lower

Commentary: Eleanor's monologue is a scolding rebuke that touches on all her husband's weaknesses. Her remarks could easily be construed as an attack on his manliness (lines 1-2). Eleanor is ambitious and haughty. Until the young King's marriage to Margaret, she had been more Queen of England than any other woman in the realm. And playing that role has given her airs.

Unfortunately, avarice and scolding are two of her dominant traits. But if she can work through and with the gentle Duke to get her way, she will. So she offers him here a chance to "reach at the glorious gold" of majesty. She literally wants to lift the Duke's horizons. All her verse lines point in that direction. She is an over-achiever who wants to overleap her position. She is also a dreamer. Elsewhere she says: "Methought I sat in seat of majesty,/In the cathedral church of Westminster." Her queenly thoughts are too much on the crown, and Queen Margaret (see below 1.3.77-89) is quick to note that Eleanor is a threat.

HENRY VI, Part 2

Queen Margaret

Act 1, Scene 3. London, The King's palace. Margaret of Anjou, who continues a secret love affair with the Duke of Suffolk, is now married to King Henry VI as part of a grand alliance which backfires. She does not even come with a dowry. Yet the King is delighted by her fierce spirit, which is set loose here on a group of fawning petitioners when she sees how corruptly the English court operates.

[QUEEN MARGARET *(to the Petitioners)*
    And as for you that love to be protected
40 Under the wings of our Protector's grace,
    Begin your suits anew and sue to him.
    (She tears the supplication)
    Away, base cullions! Suffolk, let them go.
ALL PETITIONERS Come, let's be gone.

                        Exeunt Petitioners]

QUEEN MARGARET
    My lord of Suffolk, say, is this the guise?°
45 Is this the fashions in the court of England?
    Is this the government of Britain's isle,
    And this the royalty of Albion's° king?
    What, shall King Henry be a pupil still
    Under the surly Gloucester's governance?
50 Am I a queen in title and in style,
    And must be made a subject to a duke?
    I tell thee, Pole,° when in the city Tours
    Thou rann'st a-tilt° in honor of my love
    And stol'st away the ladies' hearts of France,
55 I thought King Henry had resembled thee
    In courage, courtship, and proportion.
    But all his mind is bent to holiness,°

To number Ave-Maries on his beads.
His champions are the prophets and apostles,
60 His weapons holy saws° of sacred writ,
His study is his tilt-yard, and his loves
Are brazen° images of canonizèd saints.
I would the college of the cardinals
Would choose him Pope, and carry him to Rome,
65 And set the triple crown° upon his head—
That were a state fit for his holiness.
[SUFFOLK
Madam, be patient—as I was cause
Your highness came to England, so will I
In England work your grace's full content.]
QUEEN MARGARET
70 Beside the haught° Protector have we Beaufort
The imperious churchman, Somerset,
        Buckingham,
And grumbling York; and not the least of these
But can do more in England than the King.
[SUFFOLK
And he of these that can do most of all
75 Cannot do more in England than the Nevilles:
Salisbury and Warwick are no simple peers.]
QUEEN MARGARET
Not all these lords do vex° me half so much
As that proud dame, the Lord Protector's wife.
She sweeps it° through the court with troops of
        ladies
80 More like an empress than Duke Humphrey's wife.
Strangers in court do take her for the queen.
She bears a duke's revenues° on her back,°
And in her heart she scorns our poverty.
Shall I not live to be avenged on her?
85 Contemptuous base-born callet° as she is,
She vaunted° 'mongst her minions t'other day
The very train° of her worst-wearing gown

67

Was better worth than all my father's lands,
Till Suffolk gave two dukedoms° for his daughter.

44 **guise**/habit 47 **Albion's**/England's 52 **Pole**/Suffolk, i.e., William de le Pole 53 **rann'st a-tilt**/competed in a tournament 57 **holiness**/religion 60 **saws**/sayings, proverbs 62 **brazen**/brass 65 **triple crown**/papal crown (also sexual allusion to a cockscomb of a cuckold, perhaps) 70 **haught**/high 77 **vex**/anger 79 **sweeps it**/i.e., lords it majestically (sarcastic image like *camps it up*) 82 **revenues**/income **on her back**/i.e., in her dress 85 **callet**/whore 86 **vaunted**/exalted 87 **train**/tail 89 **two dukedoms**/(as part of the marriage negotiation, Suffolk surrended the duchies of Anjou and Maine in order to secure Margaret for Henry)

Commentary: Margaret's speeches are part rant and part exposition. She is quick to notice that the English court operates largely through the Lord Protector (Duke of Gloucester), and not through the King. The boy-King Henry is now a man, but he lacks the strong character of a ruler. Margaret has it, however, and begins to show it here. She is sharp-tongued, imperious, quick to see faults and not one bit interested in being "a subject to a duke." Though newly married, she instantly encapsulates all of Henry's weaknesses. She also lines up all the other players in the power game. The main object of her hate is Eleanor, Duchess of Gloucester (lines 77-89). We can literally hear plots begin to take shape. Margaret is one of the few Shakespeare women who speaks, thinks and acts like a man. Her presence and position in four plays (three parts of *Henry VI* and *Richard III*)—the most bitterly internecine of all the history plays—is unrivaled by any other female character. Throughout the tetralogy, she ages from being a lively young girl to a haggard old witch. One can note her bitterness in the speeches here, and the rough struggle her future promises.

HENRY VI, Part 2

Eleanor

Act 2, Scene 4. London. A street. Ambitious for the crown, Eleanor, Duchess of Gloucester, has allowed herself to become involved with witches and conjurers. But she has been set-up by Queen Margaret and Suffolk. She meets her husband, the Duke, on the way from her trial for treason.

[*Enter the Duchess, Dame Eleanor Cobham, barefoot, with a white sheet about her, written verses pinned on her back, and carrying a wax candle in her hand; she is accompanied by the two Sheriffs of London, and Sir John Stanley, and officers with bills and halberds*]

[SERVANT (*to Gloucester*)
    So please your grace, we'll take her from the
        sheriffs.
GLOUCESTER
    No, stir not for your lives, let her pass by.]
DUCHESS
20 Come you, my lord, to see my open shame?
    Now thou dost penance too. Look how they gaze,
    See how the giddy° multitude do point
    And nod their heads, and throw their eyes on thee.
    Ah, Gloucester, hide thee from their hateful looks,
25 And, in thy closet° pent up, rue° my shame,
    And ban thine enemies—both mine and thine.
[GLOUCESTER
    Be patient, gentle Nell; forget this grief.]
DUCHESS
    Ah, Gloucester, teach me to forget myself;
    For whilst I think I am thy married wife,
30 And thou a prince, Protector of this land,

Methinks I should not thus be led along,
Mailed° up in shame, with papers° on my back,
And followed with a rabble that rejoice
To see my tears and hear my deep-fet° groans.
35 The ruthless flint° doth cut my tender feet,
And when I start,° the envious people laugh,
And bid° me be advisèd° how I tread.
Ah, Humphrey, can I bear this shameful yoke?
Trowest° thou that e'er I'll look upon the world,
40 Or count them happy that enjoys the sun?
No, dark shall be my light, and night my day;
To think upon my pomp shall be my hell.
Sometime I'll say I am Duke Humphrey's wife,
And he a prince and ruler of the land;
45 Yet so he ruled, and such a prince he was,
As he stood by whilst I, his forlorn° Duchess,
Was made a wonder and a pointing stock°
To every idle rascal follower.
But be thou mild and blush not at my shame,
50 Nor stir at nothing till the axe of death
Hang over thee, as sure it shortly will.
For Suffolk,° he that can do all in all
With her that hateth thee and hates us all,
And York, and impious Beaufort that false priest,
55 Have all limed bushes° to betray thy wings,
And fly thou how thou canst, they'll tangle thee.
But fear not thou until thy foot be snared,
Nor never seek prevention of thy foes.°

22 **giddy**/fickle 25 **closet**/private apartment **rue**/regard with pity 32
Mailed/wrapped, enmeshed **papers**/i.e., listing her crimes 34 **deep-fet**/
deeply fetched 35 **flint**/i.e., stones of the street 36 **start**/flinch 37 **bid**/call
out to **be advised**/be careful 39 **Trowest**/think 46 **forlorn**/lost, destroyed
47 **pointing stock**/object of ridicule 52 **Suffolk**/Duke of Suffolk (the lover
of Queen Margaret and chief plotter against Gloucester) 55 **limed
bushes**/smeared a sticky substance to ensnare birds 58 **Nor...foes**/i.e.,
never underestimate your enemies

Commentary: Eleanor is being paraded shamefully through the streets in penitent's rags. She is as far fallen from her queenly ambitions as she could possibly be. And her whole speech is a cruel recognition of the fact that she has become a parody of pageantry: "To think upon my pomp shall be my hell." The tetralogy that comprises the three *Henry VI* plays and *Richard III* revel in such scenes of human degradation. What happens to Eleanor here will happen later to Queen Margaret as well. They are all on a treadmill of shame and their sins become spectacles in time. Her monologue is a warning and a lament. It is full of contrasting antitheses: "dark shall be my light, and night my day." The actor should also note that Eleanor, with her crimes pinned to her back, has become a walking and talking billboard. She is very much a commercial for the dangers of overleaping ambition.

HENRY VI, Part 2

Queen Margaret

Act 3, Scene 1. The abbey at Bury St. Edmunds. Queen Margaret has been plotting with her lover, the Duke of Suffolk, and others against the Lord Protector, the Duke of Gloucester. The Protector has not appeared before the King, and Margaret uses the advantage of his absence to denounce him.

QUEEN MARGARET
　　Can you not see, or will ye not observe,
5　The strangeness of his altered countenance?°
　　With what a majesty he bears himself?
　　How insolent of late he is become?
　　How proud, how peremptory,° and unlike himself?
　　We know the time since° he was mild and affable,
10　And if we did but glance a far-off look,
　　Immediately he was upon his knee,°
　　That all the court admired him for submission.
　　But meet him now, and be it in the morn
　　When everyone will give the time of day,°
15　He knits his brow, and shows an angry eye,
　　And passeth by with stiff unbowèd knee,
　　Disdaining° duty that to us belongs.
　　Small curs° are not regarded when they grin,°
　　But great men tremble when the lion roars—
20　And Humphrey is no little man in England.
　　First, note that he is near you in descent,°
　　And, should you fall, he is the next will mount.
　　Meseemeth then it is no policy,°
　　Respecting what a rancorous mind he bears
25　And his advantage following your decease,
　　That he should come about your royal person,
　　Or be admitted to your highness' Council.

By flattery hath he won the commons'° hearts,
And when he please to make commotion,
30 'Tis to be feared they all will follow him.
Now 'tis the spring, and weeds are shallow-rooted;
Suffer° them now, and they'll o'ergrow the garden,
And choke the herbs for want of husbandry.°
The reverent care I bear unto my Lord
35 Made me collect° these dangers in the Duke.
If it be fond,° call it a woman's fear;
Which fear, if better reasons can supplant,
I will subscribe° and say I wronged the Duke.
My lord of Suffolk, Buckingham, and York,
40 Reprove° my allegation if you can,
Or else conclude my words effectual.°

5 **countenance**/appearance, favor   8 **peremptory**/determined, proud, overbearing   9 **since**/when   11 **upon his knee**/i.e., kneeling in respect   14 **give...day**/say "Good morning"   17 **Disdaining**/scorning   18 **curs**/dogs   **grin**/bare their teeth   21 **descent**/line to the throne   23 **no policy**/unwise, imprudent   28 **commons'**/common peoples'   32 **Suffer**/tolerate   33 **husbandry**/proper management   35 **collect**/infer   36 **fond**/foolish, silly   38 **subscribe**/acknowledge   40 **Reprove**/disprove   41 **effectual**/as pertinent, grave

Commentary: Margaret's speech is full of political maneuverings. She plants seeds of doubt in the King's mind. The chief irony of the speech is that Gloucester, Henry's uncle, is the only *good* character in the whole play ("the map of honor, truth and loyalty"). But Margaret's monologue skillfully isolates him from the King. She can offer no specific crime with which to accuse and implicate him, so her speech is merely a catalog of vague incriminations certain to raise fears. In her list, "pride" and "insolence" are chief faults. He comes across as a *potentially* destructive weed in the King's garden kingdom. Asserting herself in the final eight lines of the verse has the effect of placing Margaret between the King and Gloucester. Typically, Margaret does *not* resort to any kind of feminine wiles to influence her husband, except at line 36. Her language is that of the political tactician, noting moves and countermoves. Her range as a Machiavellian plotter continues to enlarge. Ironically, she herself is many of the things that she accuses Gloucester of being.

HENRY VI, Part 3

Queen Margaret

Act 1, Scene 4. A battlefield near Wakefield. Queen Margaret ("stern, obdurate, flinty, rough, remorseless" "Captain Margaret") leads her troops in the capture of Richard Plantagenet, Duke of York, and pretender to King Henry's crown. She makes a spectacle of her catch before her men.

QUEEN MARGARET
    Brave warriors, Clifford and Northumberland,
    Come make him stand upon this molehill° here,
    That wrought° at mountains with outstretchèd
        arms
70 Yet parted but the shadow with his hand.
    (To York) What°—was it you that would be
        England's king?
    Was't you that revelled° in our Parliament,
    And made a preachment of your high descent?°
    Where are your mess° of sons to back you now?
75 The wanton° Edward and the lusty George?
    And where's that valiant crookback prodigy,°
    Dickie,° your boy, that with his grumbling° voice
    Was wont to cheer his dad in mutinies?
    Or with the rest where is your darling Rutland?°
80 Look, York, I stained this napkin with the blood
    That valiant Clifford with his rapier's point
    Made issue from the bosom of thy boy.
    And if thine eyes can water° for his death,
    I give thee this to dry thy cheeks withal.
85 Alas, poor York, but that ° I hate thee deadly
    I should lament thy miserable state.
    I prithee, grieve,° to make me merry, York.

74

What—hath thy fiery heart so parched thine
    entrails°
That not a tear can fall for Rutland's death?
90 Why art thou patient,° man? Thou shouldst be
    mad,
And I, to make thee mad, do mock thee thus.
Stamp, rave, and fret, that I may sing and dance.
Thou wouldst be fee'd,° I see, to make me sport.
York cannot speak unless he wear a crown.
(To her men) A crown for York, and, lords, bow
95   low to him.
Hold you his hands whilst I do set it on.
(She puts a paper crown on York's head)
Ay, marry,° sir, now looks he like a king,
Ay, this is he that took King Henry's chair,°
And this is he was his adopted heir.
100 But how is it that great Plantagenet
Is crowned so soon and broke his solemn oath?
As I bethink me, you should not be king
Till our King Henry had shook hands with death.
And will you pale° your head in Henry's glory,
105 And rob his temples of the diadem
Now, in his life, against your holy oath?
O 'tis a fault too, too, unpardonable.
Off with the crown,
(She knocks it from his head)
               and with the crown his head,
And whilst we breathe,° take time to do him dead.°

---

68 **molehill**/small hillock 69 **wrought**/reached 71 **What**/(note the pause
and room for stage business here) 72 **revelled**/proclaimed loudly 73 **high
descent**/(York claimed the crown by right of birth) 74 **mess**/set of four 75
wanton/licentious, roguish 76 **prodigy**/monster (i.e., the deformed
Richard, latter Richard III) 77 **Dickie**/Richard (also used as a sexual taunt)
grumbling/dissenting 79 **Rutland**/York's youngest son killed in battle by
Clifford (she will smear York's face with Rutland's blood) 83 **water**/cry 85
but that/except for the fact that 87 **grieve**/show grief (note the antithesis
of "grieve" and "merry") 88 **entrails**/insides 90 **patient**/(obviously York is
showing no emotion at Margaret's taunts, so she increases the level of

sadistic mockery) 93 **fee'd**/paid (like a performing animal) 97 **marry**/
indeed, how handsome 98 **chair**/throne 104 **pale**/enclose (with a crown)
109 **breathe**/rest (a breather from fighting) **do him dead**/kill him

Commentary: Queen Margaret displays a sadistic and vengeful
streak in this long spectacle of a monologue. Notice how she puts
York on a stage, the molehill, for this mock coronation. It is full of
taunts, sneers, tortures, and marvelous theatrical moments—note the
"napkin" and "paper crown." In the course of the *Henry VI* plays,
Margaret has become a superb stage manager of events like this.
Only Cleopatra is her rival at creating such theatrical moments.
She treats York like a naughty boy (lines 74-79) caught in the act of
mischief. But the actor musn't forget that Margaret's glee in
trapping her catch has, behind it, bloody intentions. She basically
says, "off with his head," in the final lines. Through much of her
speech she is simply playing the cat to York's mouse. As York says
of her at line 137, she is a "tiger's heart wrapp'd in a woman's
hide!" The cat image works well for the actor. Before she "crowns"
the soon-to-be-martyred York, she smears (annoints) his face with
the blood of his slain son. The whole display is a wicked parody of
kingly investiture. Margaret is capable of that sort of grizzly
humor. Mockery has always been one of her favorite devices.

HENRY VIII

Katherine

Act 2, Scene 4. London. A hall in Blackfriars prepared for trial. After twenty years of marriage to Katherine of Arragon, Henry VIII seeks to divorce her (on a technicality that their marriage was illegal) so that he can marry Anne Boleyn. The Queen is brought to trial and delivers this defense.

[CRIER
10 Katherine, Queen of England, come into the court.
     (The Queen makes no answer, but rises out of
     her chair, goes about the court, comes to the
     King, and kneels at his feet. Then she speaks)]
QUEEN KATHERINE
     Sir, I desire you do me right and justice,
     And to bestow your pity on me; for
15 I am a most poor woman, and a stranger,
     Born out of your dominions,° having here
     No judge indifferent,° nor no more assurance
     Of equal friendship and proceeding.° Alas, sir,
     In what have I offended you? What cause
20 Hath my behavior given to your displeasure
     That thus you should proceed to put me off,°
     And take your good grace° from me? Heaven
          witness°
     I have been to you a true and humble wife,
     At all times to your will conformable,°
25 Ever in fear to kindle your dislike,°
     Yea, subject to your countenance,° glad or sorry
     As I saw it inclined. When was the hour
     I ever contradicted your desire,
     Or made it not mine too? Or which of your friends
30 Have I not strove to love, although I knew

77

He were mine enemy? What friend of mine
That had to him derived° your anger did I
Continue in my liking? Nay, gave notice
He was from thence discharged? Sir, call to mind°
35 That I have been your wife in this obedience
Upward of twenty years, and have been blessed
With many children by you. If, in the course
And process of this time, you can report—
And prove it, too—against mine honor aught,°
40 My bond to wedlock, or my love and duty
Against your sacred person, in God's name
Turn me away, and let the foul'st contempt
Shut door upon me, and so give me up
To the sharp'st kind of justice. Please you, sir,
45 The King your father was reputed° for
A prince most prudent, of an excellent
And unmatched wit and judgement. Ferdinand
My Father, King of Spain, was reckoned one°
The wisest prince that there had reigned by many
50 A year before. It is not to be questioned
That they had gathered a wise council to them
Of every realm, that did debate this business,
Who deemed our marriage lawful. Wherefore I
    humbly
Beseech you, sir, to spare me till I may
55 Be by my friends in Spain advised, whose counsel
I will implore. If not, i'th' name of God,
Your pleasure be fulfilled.

16 **dominions**/territories 17 **indifferent**/unbiased, impartial 18 **proceeding**/i.e., due process of law 21 **put me off**/reject me, divorce 22 **good
grace**/good self **Heaven witness**/i.e., as God is my witness 24 **conform-
able**/compliant, submissive 25 **dislike**/displeasure 26 **countenance**/
favor 32 **derived**/incurred 34 **call to mind**/remember 39 **aught**/
anything 45 **reputed**/reported 48 **one**/one of

Commentary: Katherine is one of the purest and most noble of
Shakespeare's mature heroines. Lacking a defense from anyone else,

she speaks on her own behalf to a fully assembled group of judges, spectators and the King. Those in attendance are all men. Katherine's defense is eloquent, and based on her faithful execution of all her wifely duties. The first half of the verse is full of questions that ask for proof and witness of her flaws. Her whole argument has legal weight behind it, and she even invokes, as kinds of character witnesses, the King's father and her own. Threading back through the speech, however, one notes Katherine's weaknesses: she is a woman and a stranger in England (line 15). So skilled is Katherine at legal manuevering, however, she will eventually refuse being tried in this manner and ask for a trial before the Pope. Twenty years has taught her that a queen cannot be deposed so easily. Notice how steady, regular and solid is her verse.

JULIUS CAESAR

Portia

Act 2, Scene 1. Rome. Brutus' garden on the night before the assassination of Julius Caesar. Portia tries to comfort her brooding husband, Brutus.

[BRUTUS
    Portia, what mean you? Wherefore rise you now?
235 It is not for your health thus to commit
    Your weak condition to the raw cold morning.]
PORTIA
                    You've ungently,° Brutus,
    Stole from my bed; and yesternight at supper
    You suddenly arose, and walked about
240 Musing and sighing, with your arms across;°
    And when I asked you what the matter was,
    You stared upon me with ungentle looks.
    I urged you further; then you scratched your head,
    And too impatiently stamped with your foot.
245 Yet I insisted; yet you answered not,
    But with an angry wafture° of your hand
    Gave sign for me to leave you. So I did,
    Fearing to strengthen that impatience
    Which seemed too much enkindled, and withal°
250 Hoping it was but an effect of humor,°
    Which sometime hath his hour° with every man.
    It will not let you eat, nor talk, nor sleep;
    And could it work so much upon your shape°
    As it hath much prevailed on your condition,°
255 I should not know you Brutus. Dear my lord,
    Make me acquainted with° your cause of grief.
[BRUTUS
    I am not well in health, and that is all.]

PORTIA

    Brutus is wise, and were he not in health
    He would embrace the means to come by it.°

[BRUTUS

260 Why, so I do. Good Portia, go to bed.]

PORTIA

    Is Brutus sick? And is it physical°
    To walk unbracèd° and suck up the humors°
    Of the dank° morning? What, is Brutus sick?
    And will he steal out of his wholesome bed

265 To dare the vile contagion° of the night,
    And tempt the rheumy° and unpurgèd° air
    To add unto his sickness? No, my Brutus,
    You have some sick offence° within your mind,
    Which by the right and virtue of my place°

270 I ought to know of. (*Kneeling*) And upon my
       knees,
    I charm° you by my once-commended beauty,
    By all your vows of love, and that great vow
    Which did incorporate° and make us one,
    That you unfold° to me, your self, your half,°

275 Why you are heavy,° and what men tonight
    Have had resort° to you—for here have been
    Some six or seven, who did hide their faces
    Even from darkness.

[BRUTUS   Kneel not, gentle Portia.]

PORTIA (*rising*)

    I should not need if you were gentle Brutus.

280 Within the bond of marriage, tell me, Brutus,
    Is it excepted° I should know no secrets
    That appertain to you? Am I your self
    But as it were in sort or limitation?°
    To keep with you at meals, comfort your bed,

285 And talk to you sometimes? Dwell I but in the
       suburbs°

Of your good pleasure? If it be no more,
Portia is Brutus' harlot,° not his wife.

237 **ungently**/disrespectfully   240 **across**/folded across (sign of melancholy)   246 **angry wafture**/dismissive wave   249 **withal**/besides   250 **humor**/ill mood   251 **his hour**/its time   253 **shape**/outward appearance   254 **condition**/disposition   256 **Make...with**/i.e., confide in me   259 **means ...it**/means to get well   261 **physical**/healthy   262 **unbracèd**/with doublet open   **humors**/moisture   263 **dank**/damp   265 **contagion**/infected night air   266 **rheumy**/damp   **unpurged**/i.e., not yet purified by the morning sun   268 **offence**/hurt   269 **place**/position   as your wife   271 **charm**/solemnly entreat   273 **incorporate**/unite as one body *(corpus)*   274 **unfold**/disclose   **half**/other half, wife   275 **heavy**/melancholy   276 **had resort**/visited   281 **excepted**/made an exception   283 **in sort or limitation**/conditionally (legal terms)   285 **suburbs**/i.e., the environs where prostitutes live   287 **harlot**/whore

Commentary: Portia's imploring speech is a reflection of Brutus' anxiety. As his other "half," the sickly Portia must reveal all the feeling and worry that Brutus' Roman side cannot express. She takes exceeding care to note all the physical and mental discomforts he will not openly articulate. The emotional intensity that she voices is in direct counterpoint to the cold political calculation of Cassius and the other "six or seven, who did hide their faces/Even from darkness." Her continual questions show that she gets no answers from the sanguine Brutus. She even invokes legal rights to get a response (lines 280-283). Her final line, "Portia is Brutus' harlot, not his wife," is delivered in exasperation and probably some anger. Later in the play, we hear that she has committed suicide out of grief.

JULIUS CAESAR

Calpurnia

*Act 2, Scene 2. Rome. Caesar's house at night.
Calpurnia enters to try and prevent Caesar from leaving home at daybreak. She has had nightmares of
Caesar's murder and here tells him of these portents.*

CALPURNIA
What mean you,° Caesar? Think you to walk
    forth?
You shall not stir out of your house today.
[CAESAR
10 Caesar shall forth. The things that threatened me
Ne'er looked but on my back; when they shall see
The face of Caesar, they are vanishèd.]
CALPURNIA
Caesar, I never stood on ceremonies,°
Yet now they fright me. There is one° within,
15 Besides the things that we have heard and seen,
Recounts most horrid sights seen by the watch.°
A lioness hath whelpèd° in the streets,
And graves have yawned° and yielded up their
    dead.
Fierce fiery warriors fight° upon the clouds,
20 In ranks and squadrons and right form of war,°
Which drizzled blood upon the Capitol.
The noise of battle hurtled° in the air.
Horses do neigh, and dying men did groan,
And ghosts° did shriek and squeal about the streets.
25 O Caesar, these things are beyond all use,°
And I do fear them.
[CAESAR What can be avoided
Whose end is purposed by the mighty gods?
Yet Caesar shall go forth, for these predictions

Are to the world in general as to Caesar.]
CALPURNIA
30   When beggars die there are no comets seen;
     The heavens themselves blaze forth° the death of
     princes.

8 **What mean you**/what are you doing   13 **stood on ceremonies**/placed importance in omens   14 **one**/i.e., an officer, perhaps   16 **watch**/night guard   17 **whelpèd**/given birth   18 **yawned**/opened   19 **fight**/(note the sound string of *fierce, fiery, fight*)   20 **right form of war**/battle formation   22 **hurtled**/clashed   24 **ghosts**/(begins a sound string with *shriek, squeal, streets*)   25 **use**/usual experience   31 **blaze forth**/proclaim, i.e., like a comet or falling star (in keeping with portents)

Commentary: Calpurnia's speech mirrors that of Portia to Brutus (above 2.1). But her sleep has been even more fitful with portents of Caesar's assassination later that day. She is not nearly as close to the cold Caesar as Portia is to the more gentle Brutus. The most vivid parts of her speech are the frightening images that she parades like a series of visual projections. Her visions are Cassandra-like in the doom they foretell. Often, Shakespeare's women have a visionary capacity that is greater than any of his men. They make up for their lack of action by retreating to a world of nightmares, visions and madness. And so the actor must give careful focus to the horrors that the character conjures in language. Her speech is meant to frighten and block Caesar. But he is too cold to be stopped.

KING JOHN

Constance

Act 2, Scene 2.   France.   The French King Philip's pavilion.   Lady Constance, widow of Geoffrey, King John's brother, and mother of Arthur, John's rival to the throne, becomes distraught when Salisbury tells her of the planned dynastic marriage between the French Dauphin Louis and Blanche of Spain.   The move blocks her son's advance to the crown.

CONSTANCE *(to Salisbury)*
Gone to be married? Gone to swear a peace?
False blood° to false blood joined! Gone to be
    friends?°
Shall Louis have Blanche, and Blanche those
    provinces?
It is not so, thou hast misspoke, misheard.
5   Be well advised, tell o'er° thy tale again.
It cannot be, thou dost but say 'tis so.
I trust I may not trust thee, for thy word
Is but the vain breath of a common° man.
Believe me, I do not believe thee, man;
10   I have a king's oath to the contrary.
Thou shalt be punished for thus frighting me;
For I am sick and capable of° fears;
Oppressed with wrongs, and therefore full of fears;
A widow husbandless, subject to fears;
15   A woman naturally born to fears;
And though thou now confess thou didst but jest,
With my vexed spirits I cannot take a truce,°
But they will quake and tremble all this day.
What dost thou mean by shaking of thy head?
20   Why dost thou look so sadly on my son?
What means that hand upon that breast of thine?

Why holds thine eye that lamentable rheum,°
Like a proud river peering o'er his bounds?
Be these sad signs confirmers of thy words?
25 Then speak again—not all thy former tale,
But this one word: whether thy tale be true.

2 false blood/unlawful pretenders to the crown friends/lovers 5 o'er/over
8 common/vulgar 12 capable of/susceptible to 17 take a truce/make a
peace 22 lamentable rheum/sad tears

Commentary: Lady Constance's emotional harangue is delivered
as a string of angry declarations. The news is so sudden and amaz-
ing, like all the early reversals in *King John*, she cannot contain her
disbelief (lines 1-10). She has been plotting in one direction for her
son Arthur; now events are on a totally different path. The irony is
that the king's "oath" (line 10) is as empty as the air. Half way
through the speech her litany of fears surface, and the word "fear"
echoes and punctuates each line. When she sees Salisbury "shaking" his head (line 19), she can tell all is lost. Her woe becomes a
bit comic, but she rages on. And rage and hysterical defense of her
son are her motivations throughout the play. A weak and "pretty"
boy, Arthur needs someone like Constance to fight his battles and
stand up for his rights. Towards the end of *King John*, we will hear
that Constance has "in a frenzy died."

KING JOHN

Constance

Act 2, Scene 2. France. The French King Philip's pavilion. Enraged at the news of the French Dauphin Louis' betrothal to Blanche of Spain, Constance turns her anger towards her son Arthur, King John's rival to the English throne.

[ARTHUR
    I do beseech you, madam, be content.]
CONSTANCE
    If thou that° bidd'st me be content wert grim,
    Ugly and sland'rous° to thy mother's womb,
45 Full of unpleasing blots and sightless° stains,
    Lame, foolish,° crooked, swart,° prodigious,°
    Patched with foul moles and eye-offending marks,
    I would not care, I then would be content,
    For then I should not love thee, no, nor thou
50 Become thy great birth, nor deserve a crown.
    But thou art fair,° and at thy birth, dear boy,
    Nature and Fortune joined to make thee great.°
    Of Nature's gifts thou mayst with lilies boast,
    And with the half-blown° rose. But Fortune, O,
55 She is corrupted, changed, and won from thee;
    Sh'adulterates° hourly with thine uncle John,
    And with her golden hand hath plucked on France
    To tread down° fair respect of sovereignty,
    And made his majesty the bawd to theirs.
60 France is a bawd to Fortune and King John,
    That strumpet° Fortune, that usurping° John.
    [*(To Salisbury)* Tell me, thou fellow, is not France
        forsworn?
    Envenom him with words, or get thee gone
    And leave those woes alone, which I alone

Am bound to underbear.
SALISBURY
65 Pardon me, madam,
    I may not go without you to the Kings.
CONSTANCE
    Thou mayst, thou shalt; I will not go with thee.]
    I will instruct° my sorrows to be proud,
    For grief is proud and makes his owner stoop.°
    (She sits upon the ground)
70 To me and to the state of my great grief
    Let kings assemble,° for my grief's so great
    That no supporter but the huge firm earth
    Can hold it up. Here I and sorrows sit;
    Here is my throne; bid kings come bow to it.

43 **that**/who 44 **sland'rous**/disgraceful 45 **sightless**/unsightly 46 **foolish**/
lunatic **swart**/dark, swarthy **prodigious**/abnormal 51 **fair**/handsome
(Arthur is a "pretty" boy) 52 **great**/i.e., in line to be king 54 **half-blown**/half
bloomed 56 **adulterates**/commits adultery 58 **tread down**/trample (her
images are drawn from gardening) 61 **strumpet**/whore **usurping**/
pretender 68 **instruct**/teach, inform 69 **stoop**/bow under its weight 70-71
To...assemble/i.e., let the great come to me to honor my grief

Commentary: Constance continues her earlier harangue by taking
out her wrath on Arthur, who unluckily gets in her way. She spews
out a litany of insults (lines 43-47), all facial images, that are
certainly not the language of a lady, or of a mother. But the words
are in high contrast to the more loving phrases that follow (lines
50-54). So many characters in *King John* are at the mercy of
Fortune's turning wheel. Constance and Arthur are among the most
luckless. In her mind, Lady Fortune is a right whore, dallying with
the treacherous King John. Constance is one of those grieving female
characters in Shakespeare who love to wear sorrow like a great,
heavy costume. And the weight of her gown of grief is so burden-
some "That no supporter but the huge firm earth/Can hold it up." It
even forces her to the ground.

KING JOHN

Constance

Act 3, Scene 1. France. The French King Philip's pavilion. Louis the Dauphin of France and Lady Blanche of Spain have just been wedded. All the nobles of the different factions enter to celebrate. Lady Constance disrupts the festivities with her outburst.

CONSTANCE
  A wicked day, and not a holy day!
10 What hath this day deserved? What hath it done,
  That it in golden° letters should be set
  Among the high tides° in the calendar?
  Nay, rather turn this day out of the week,
  This day of shame, oppression, perjury.
15 Or if it must stand still,° let wives with child°
  Pray that their burdens may not fall this day,
  Lest that their hopes prodigiously° be crossed;
  But on this day let seamen fear no wreck;
  No bargains break that are not this day made;
20 This day all things begun come to ill end,
  Yea, faith itself to hollow falsehood change.°
[KING PHILIP
  By heaven, lady, you shall have no cause
  To curse the fair proceedings of this day.
  Have I not pawned to you my majesty?]
CONSTANCE
25 You have beguiled me with a counterfeit°
  Resembling majesty, which being touched° and
      tried
  Proves valueless. You are forsworn, forsworn.
  You came in arms to spill mine enemies' blood,
  But now in arms you strengthen it with yours.
30 The grappling vigor and rough frown of war

89

Is cold in amity and painted° peace,
And our oppression hath made up this league.°
Arm, arm, you heavens, against these perjured°
   Kings!
A widow cries, be husband to me, God!
35 Let not the hours of this ungodly day
Wear out the day in peace, but ere° sun set
Set armèd discord 'twixt these perjured Kings.
Hear me, O hear me!
[AUSTRIA   Lady Constance, peace.]
CONSTANCE
War, war, no peace! Peace is to me a war.
40 O Limoges, O Austria, thou dost shame
That bloody spoil. Thou slave, thou wretch, thou
   coward!
Thou little valiant, great in villainy;
Thou ever strong upon the stronger side;
Thou Fortune's champion, that dost never fight
45 But when her humorous ladyship is by
To teach thee safety. Thou art perjured too,
And sooth'st up° greatness. What a fool art thou,
A ramping° fool, to brag and stamp, and swear
Upon my party! Thou cold-blooded slave,
50 Hast thou not spoke like thunder on my side,
Been sworn my soldier, bidding me depend
Upon thy stars,° thy fortune, and thy strength?
And dost thou now fall over to my foes?
Thou wear a lion's hide! Doff° it, for shame,
55 And hang a calf's-skin° on those recreant° limbs.

---

11 **golden**/rich 12 **high tides**/feast days 15 **stand still**/remain **with
child**/pregnant 17 **prodigiously**/monstrously 21 **change**/transform 25
counterfeit/false promise 26 **touched**/tested (on a touchstone for its gold
content) 31 **painted**/unreal, imitation 32 **league**/alliance 33 **perjured**/
lying 36 **ere**/before 47 **sooth'st up**/flatters up to 48 **ramping**/stamping,
raging 52 **stars**/fortune 54 **Doff**/uncover 55 **calf's skin**/i.e., indicating
meekness **recreant**/cowardly

Commentary: Constance, still raging over the news of this marriage, delivers a series of biting curses on the "holy day" and then on the assembled kings. Her earlier anger had moments of comic potential. But here her string of epithets, or oaths, begins to wear thin and show the strain she is under. In a world of duplicity, Constance is out of place. She has one theme, her son. Anything that goes against her focus is a lie. Anyone who speaks to her is suddenly the object of her wrath. Note how the interjections of King Philip and Austria turn her rage in their direction. She is clearly a whirlwind out of control onstage. Immediately after this three part speech, King Philip aptly says to her: "You are as fond of grief as of your child." And that is a pretty fair estimate of both Constance and her motivation.

KING JOHN

Constance

Act 3, Scene 4.   France.   The French King Philip's pavilion.   New broils have broken out between members of the warring factions.   King John takes Arthur prisoner, and will soon have him murdered. Lady Constance, her hair unbound, enters in grief.

CONSTANCE
    Yes, that I will. And wherefore will I do it
70 I tore them from their bonds, and cried aloud,
    "O that these hands could so redeem my son,
    As they have given these hairs their liberty!"
    But now I envy at their liberty,
    And will again commit them to their bonds,
75 Because my poor child is a prisoner.
    (She binds up her hair)
    And Father Cardinal, I have heard you say
    That we shall see and know our friends in heaven.
    If that be true, I shall see my boy again;
    For since the birth of Cain, the first male child,
80 To him that did but yesterday suspire,°
    There was not such a gracious creature born.
    But now will canker-sorrow° eat my bud,
    And chase the native beauty° from his cheek;
    And he will look as hollow as a ghost,
85 As dim and meagre as an ague's° fit,
    And so he'll die; and rising so again,
    When I shall meet him in the court of heaven,
    I shall not know him; therefore never, never
    Must° I behold my pretty Arthur more.
[PANDOLF
90 You hold too heinous a respect of grief.]

92

CONSTANCE
    He talks to me that never had a son.
[KING PHILIP
    You are as fond of grief as of your child.]
CONSTANCE
    Grief° fills the room up of my absent child,
    Lies in his bed, walks up and down with me,
95 Puts on his pretty looks, repeats his words,
    Remembers° me of all his gracious parts,
    Stuffs out his vacant garments with his form;
    Then have I reason to be fond of grief.
    Fare you well. Had you such a loss as I,
100 I could give better comfort than you do.
    (She unbinds her hair)
    I will not keep this form° upon my head
    When there is such disorder in my wit.°
    O Lord, my boy, my Arthur, my fair son,
    My life, my joy, my food, my all the world,
105 My widow-comfort, and my sorrow's cure!

80 **suspire**/breathe 82 **canker-sorrow**/canker worm 83 **beauty**/(Arthur was noted for his beauty) 85 **ague**/fever 89 **Must**/can 93 **Grief**/ (personified here; it also shows the vivid strength and attachment of Constance's memory of Arthur 96 **Remembers**/reminds 101 **form**/order 102 **wit**/reason

Commentary: With each of her speeches, the intensity of Constance's grief swells and turns to madness. In this speech, she knows full well that her son Arthur faces certain death by King John's order. Her talk is full of ghostly images and mourning. In a way, Constance luxuriates in her grief in the same way that she held her son fast. Note what King Philip says: "You are as fond of grief as of your child." And indeed, grief becomes a personified character; something like a new-found child (lines 93-95). That kind of image gives the actor a good focus. For the Elizabethan, loose unbound hair signified a madwoman. Constance, who later dies of madness, is certainly close to it here. The hair is another strong point of acting concentration. Once loosened again at the end of the speech, a new litany of grief floods out.

KING LEAR

Goneril

Act 1, Scene 4. Britain. The Duke of Albany's palace.
Lear has given away equal halves of his kingdom to his
daughters Goneril and Regan. He is now staying with
Goneril and her husband, Albany. Goneril chides Lear
for the size of his retinue. She wants them out.

[LEAR

How now, daughter? What makes that frontlet
    on?
You are too much of late i'th' frown.

FOOL Thou wast a pretty fellow when thou hadst no
175 need to care for her frowning. Now thou art an O
without a figure. I am better than thou art, now. I
am a fool; thou art nothing. *(To Goneril)* Yes,
forsooth, I will hold my tongue; so your face bids
me, though you say nothing.
    (Sings)   Mum, mum.
180   He that keeps nor crust nor crumb,
                Weary of all, shall want some.
That's a shelled peascod.]

GONERIL *(to Lear)*

Not only, sir, this your all-licensed° fool,
But other° of your insolent retinue
185 Do hourly carp° and quarrel, breaking forth
In rank° and not-to-be-endurèd riots. Sir,
I had thought by making this well known unto you
To have found a safe redress,° but now grow
    fearful,
By what yourself too late° have spoke and done,
190 That you protect this course, and put it on°
By your allowance;° which if you should, the fault
Would not scape censure,° nor the redresses sleep°

94

Which in the tender of° a wholesome weal°
Might in their working do you that offence,
195 Which else were shame, that then necessity
Will call discreet proceeding.°
[FOOL *(to Lear)* For, you know, nuncle,
    (Sings)   The hedge-sparrow fed the cuckoo so long
                That it's had it head bit off by it young;
200 so out went the candle, and we were left darkling.
LEAR *(to Goneril)* Are you our daughter?]
GONERIL
    I would you would make use of your good wisdom,
    Whereof I know you are fraught,° and put away
    These dispositions° which of late transport you
205 From what you rightly are.
[FOOL May not an ass know when the cart draws the
    horse? *(Sings)* "Whoop, jug, I love thee!"
LEAR
    Does any here know me? This is not Lear.
    Does Lear walk thus, speak thus? Where are his
        eyes?
210 Either his notion weakens, his discernings
    Are lethargied—ha, waking? 'Tis not so.
    Who is it that can tell me who I am?
FOOL Lear's shadow.
LEAR *(to Goneril)* Your name, fair gentlewoman?]
GONERIL
215 This admiration,° sir, is much o'th' savor°
    Of other your° new pranks. I do beseech you
    To understand my purposes aright,
    As you are old and reverend, should be wise.
    Here do you keep a hundred knights and squires,
220 Men so disordered, so debauched and bold
    That this our court, infected with their manners,°
    Shows like° a riotous inn. Epicurism° and lust°
    Makes it more like a tavern or a brothel
    Than a graced° palace. The shame itself doth speak

225 For instant remedy. Be then desired,°
By her that else will take the thing she begs,
A little to disquantity° your train,°
And the remainders that shall still depend°
To be such men as may besort° your age,
230 Which know° themselves and you.

183 **all-licensed**/at liberty to say anything 184 **other**/others 185 **carp**/
complain 186 **rank**/gross, offensive 188 **redress**/relief from trouble 189
too late/lately, recently 190 **put it on**/promote it 191 **allowance**/approval
192 **censure**/unfavorable opinion **redresses sleep**/corrections fail to
follow 193 **tender of**/care for **weal**/state, commonweal 195-196 **Which...**
proceeding/(essentially she says, "My way is the right way") 203 **fraught**/
endowed, full 204 **dispositions**/moods 215 **admiration**/wonderment
savor/character, style 216 **other your**/others of your 221 **manners**/
behavior 222 **Shows like**/appears like **Epicurism**/pursuit of pleasure
lust/pleasure (sexual) 224 **graced**/distinguished, blessed 225 **desired**/
requested 227 **disquantify**/reduce in number **train**/followers, troops 228
depend/be dependent on you 229 **besort**/befits 230 **know**/i.e., know their
place and your needs

Commentary: Goneril's speeches to her father follow a fairly
strict pattern of meter. Her use of "sir" formalizes her phrasing, but
it also adds touches of sarcasm. She is clearly in charge of her house
and queenly in her addresses. The verbs and nouns she employs in
lines 184-186 speak of confusion and are bracketed by her "sirs." Her
intention is to reduce Lear's retinue and make that reduction a
foregone conclusion by the end of her speeches. At line 215 her tact
changes to one of loving concern. Her tones are more honeyed and
softened so that she can deliver her fatal blow: "to disquantify your
train." Goneril is a woman who does not falter. Her intentions are
clear and unwavering. Lear's protests only harden her. We must
never forget that she herself will later commit villainies not unlike
those she mentions here.

MACBETH

Lady Macbeth

Act 1, Scene 5. Inverness. Macbeth's castle. Lady Macbeth makes her first entrance in the play, reading a letter from Macbeth. In it he writes of the witches prophecy that he will become king. She is immediately struck by the news and her own ambitions.

LADY MACBETH *(reading)*

"They met me in the day of success,° and I have
learned by the perfect'st report° they have more in
them than mortal knowledge. When I burned in
desire to question them further, they made
5 themselves air, into which they vanished. Whiles
I stood rapt in the wonder of it came missives°
from the King, who all-hailed me 'Thane of
Cawdor,' by which title before these weird sisters°
saluted me, and referred me to the coming on of
10 time with 'Hail, King that shalt be!' This have I
thought good to deliver° thee, my dearest partner
of greatness, that thou mightst not lose the dues° of
rejoicing by being ignorant of what greatness is
promised thee. Lay it to thy heart, and farewell."
15 Glamis° thou art, and Cawdor, and shalt be
What thou art promised. Yet do I fear thy nature.
It is too full o'th' milk of human kindness°
To catch the nearest way.° Thou wouldst be great,
Art not without ambition, but without
20 The illness° should attend it. What thou wouldst
        highly,
That wouldst thou holily; wouldst not play false,
And yet wouldst wrongly win. Thou'dst have,
        great Glamis,

That which cries "Thus thou must do" if thou have
    it,
And that which rather thou dost fear to do
25 Than wishest should be undone. Hie° thee hither,
That I may pour my spirits° in thine ear
And chastise with the valor° of my tongue
All that impedes thee from the golden round°
Which fate and metaphysical° aid doth seem
30 To have thee crowned withal.°

1 **day of success**/i.e., after Macbeth's victory over the rebellious
Macdonwald, whose title of Thane of Cawdor is given to Macbeth as a
reward   2 **perfect'st report**/most reliable information   6 **missives**/
messages   8 **weird sisters**/var., *wayward*, perverted witches   11 **deliver**/
report to   12 **dues**/rights   15 **Glamis**/ Macbeth's inherited title from his
father Sinel   17 **milk...kindness**/human gentleness (used here, dis-
paragingly, to mean soft and woman-like)   18 **nearest way**/shortest route
(to power)   20 **illness**/evil, wickedness   25 **Hie**/hasten   26 **spirits**/
sentiments, feelings   27 **valor**/bravery   28 **golden round**/crown   29 **metaphysical**/supernatural   30 **withal**/with

Commentary: Lady Macbeth is full of the powerful ambitions
that her husband lacks. And it is she who will plot the murder of
King Duncan and begin the rampage of crimes that will lead
Macbeth to the throne. But, as she says, Macbeth is a weak vessel;
his nature "is too full of o'th' milk of human kindness/To catch the
nearest way." In a sense, Lady Macbeth is weak, too, and must act
through her husband. Her words and thoughts are far more callow
and wicked than her deeds. She is the "spirit" of evil, not unlike
the witches who she grows to resemble. But Macbeth is the doer.
Once Duncan is murdered by Macbeth, Lady Macbeth begins a
gradual slide into madness over the crime. What is surprising in her
speech is her quickness and certainty that the crown ("the golden
round") is within grasp. She never questions that belief for a second.
The verse lines have a nimbleness—note her "Hie thee hither"—
which underscore her sudden resolve.

MACBETH

Lady Macbeth

Act 1, Scene 5. Inverness. Macbeth's castle. Knowing that Macbeth is on his way home from battle, Lady Macbeth receives further word that King Duncan of Scotland will also be coming that night. The plan to kill Duncan takes on immediacy and dark resolve.

LADY MACBETH

> The raven° himself is hoarse
> That croaks the fatal° entrance of Duncan
> 40 Under my battlements. Come, you spirits
> That tend° on mortal° thoughts, unsex° me here,
> And fill me from the crown to the toe top-full
> Of direst cruelty. Make thick° my blood,
> Stop up th'access and passage to remorse,°
> 45 That no compunctious° visitings of nature
> Shake my fell° purpose, nor keep peace between
> Th'effect° and it. Come to my woman's breasts,
> And take my milk for gall,° you murd'ring
> ministers,°
> Wherever in your sightless° substances
> 50 You wait on nature's mischief. Come, thick° night,
> And pall thee° in the dunnest° smoke of hell,
> That my keen° knife see not the wound it makes,
> Nor heaven peep through the blanket of the dark
> To cry "Hold, Hold!"°

38 **raven**/black bird of prey that cackles 39 **fatal**/deadly 41 **tend**/attend **mortal**/deathly, murderous **unsex**/neuter, i.e., abolish all feminine sentiments 43 **thick**/heavy, cold 44 **remorse**/compassion 45 **compunctious**/remorseful 46 **fell**/savage 47 **effect**/result 48 **for gall**/in exchange for bitter cruelty **minister**/agents, spirits 49 **sightless**/invisible 50 **thick**/heavy, dark 51 **pall thee**/wrap yourself **dunnest**/grey-brown color 52 **keen**/sharp 54 **Hold**/stop, hold one's hand (a command to a criminal)

Commentary: Lady Macbeth's soliloquy is in the form of an invocation to evil spirits. In a play so full of weird forebodings and witchcraft, this speech has both in concentrated form. A string of imperatives, that begin with "Come," "Make," "Shake," take the actor through a series of conjuring moments. Lady Macbeth is also creating the right dark atmosphere and mood in which to act. She is literally transforming herself in this speech, changing herself into a witch. Note that the whole speech is self-referring with its repetitious "me" and "my." Like a scene out of a horror film, she actually goes through the motions of the murder (lines 51-54) in the same way that Macbeth will do in one of his soliloquies. The incantatory structure of the verse puts the actor at the mercy of the imperatives as if they were a series of commands and hypnotic spells. By the time Macbeth enters at line 54, Lady Macbeth can turn and speak to him as her new character. Throughout the speech she denies nature in favor of the unnatural.

MACBETH

Lady Macbeth

Act 5, Scene 1. Dunsinane. Macbeth's castle at night. This sleep walking scene of Lady Macbeth's is her last appearance in the play. Haunted by the guilt of her crimes and psychologically drained, she is watched by her lady-in-waiting and the Doctor.

(Enter Lady Macbeth with a taper)
[Lo you, here she comes. This is her very guise,° and, upon my life, fast asleep. Observe her. Stand close.°

DOCTOR
20 How came she by that light?

GENTLEWOMAN Why, it stood by her. She has light by her continually. 'Tis her command.

DOCTOR You see her eyes are open.

GENTLEWOMAN Ay, but their sense° are shut.

DOCTOR
25 What is it she does now? Look how she rubs her hands

GENTLEWOMAN It is an accustomed action with her, to seem thus washing her hands. I have known her continue in this a quarter of an hour.]

LADY MACBETH
30 Yet here's a spot.°

[DOCTOR Hark, she speaks. I will set down what comes from her to satisfy° my remembrance the more strongly.]

LADY MACBETH Out, damned spot; out I say. One, two;—why, then 'tis time to do't. Hell is murky.
35 Fie, my lord, fie, a soldier and afeard? What need

we fear who knows it when none can call our
power° to° account? Yet who would have thought
the old man to have had so much blood in him?°
[DOCTOR Do you mark that?]
LADY MACBETH
40   The Thane of Fife had a wife. Where is she now?
What, will these hands ne'er be clean? No more o'
that, my lord, no more o' that. You mar all with
this starting.°
[DOCTOR Go to, go to! You have known what you
45   should not.
GENTLEWOMAN She has spoke what she should not, I
am sure of that. Heaven knows what she has
known.]
LADY MACBETH Here's the smell of the blood still.
All the perfumes of Arabia will not sweeten this
50   little hand. O, O, O!
[DOCTOR What a sigh is there! The heart is sorely
charged,°
GENTLEWOMAN I would not have such a heart in my
bosom for the dignity of the whole body.
DOCTOR Well, well, well.
GENTLEWOMAN
55   Pray God it be, sir.
DOCTOR This disease is beyond my practice.° Yet I have
known those which have walked in their sleep
who have died holily in their beds.]
LADY MACBETH Wash your hands, put on your
60   nightgown, look not so pale. I tell you yet again,
Banquo's buried.° He cannot come out on's° grave.
[DOCTOR Even so?]
LADY MACBETH To bed, to bed! There's knocking at
the gate. Come, come, come, come, give me your
65   hand. What's done cannot be undone. To bed, to
bed, to bed!°
         (Exit)

Lady Macbeth   MACBETH

18 guise/custom 19 close/out of sight 24 sense/powers of sight 30
spot/stain, disgrace, sin 32 satisfy/confirm 37 power/i.e., because of our
position to/into 33-38 Out...him/(typical of this prose speech are the
spurts of the sentence fragments that refer to many things simultaneously)
43 starting/sudden movements 51 charged/burdened, accused 56
practice/professional skill 60-61 I...buried/(refers to the ghostly appearance
of Banquo at the banquet scene) 61 on's/of his 63-65 To bed...to
bed!/(refers to scene right after murder of Duncan)

Commentary: Lady Macbeth is totally oblivious to the presence
of onlookers. Her actions and stream of consciousness speeches
constitute a soliloquy of their own. On the verge of madness and
"sorely charged" with her crimes, she relives in unordered fragments the most intense moments of the criminal acts she has plotted
with Macbeth: the blood murder of King Duncan, the staining of her
hands with his blood, the washing of the bloody knife used in the
murder, and the subsequent murder of Macbeth's rival Banquo. She
is directed by her dreams. Only in her twilight state can Lady
Macbeth experience the full weight of guilt and remorse. As
Macbeth's power and blood lust have grown throughout the action,
Lady Macbeth has been pushed to the periphery of the play and
has not even appeared for a whole act and more. Here she is
reduced to the state of a condemned witch: in a nightgown, carrying
a taper, performing spells and uttering nonsense fragments ("The
Thane of Fife had a wife"). The hand washing action is the most
powerful physical activity in the scene. In it she re-captures Act 2,
Scene 2. Perhaps the only other scene in Shakespeare to equal this
in impact is the similar entry of mad Ophelia in *Hamlet*. Yet the
latter is driven mad by innocence and confusion, and Lady Macbeth
by guilt and nightmares. Later in the act she will die as a result of
these "thick-coming fancies."

MERCHANT OF VENICE

Portia

Act 3, Scene 2. Venice. Portia's house. Bassanio, a suitor of the wealthy heiress Portia, has just opened the leaden casket to find her portrait. As a result, he wins her hand for marriage. Portia speaks of herself as his prize.

PORTIA

You see me, Lord Bassanio, where I stand,
150 Such as I am. Though for myself alone
    I would not be ambitious in my wish
    To wish myself much better, yet for you
    I would be trebled° twenty times myself,
    A thousand times more fair, ten thousand times
        more rich,
155 That only to stand high in your account°
    I might in virtues, beauties, livings,° friends,
    Exceed account.° But the full sum° of me
    Is sum of something which, to term° in gross,
    Is an unlessoned girl, unschooled, unpractisèd,
160 Happy in this, she is not yet so old
    But she° may learn; happier than this,
    She is not bred so dull but she can learn;
    Happiest of all is that her gentle spirit
    Commits itself to yours to be directed
165 As from her lord, her governor, her king.
    Myself and what is mine to you and yours
    Is now converted.° But now° I was the lord
    Of this fair mansion, master of my servants,
    Queen o'er myself; and even now, but now,
170 This house, these servants, and this same myself
    Are yours, my lord's. I give them with this ring,
    Which when you part from, lose, or give away,

Let it presage° the ruin of your love,
And be my vantage° to exclaim on° you.

153 **trebled**/tripled 155 **account**/esteem, estimation (each of Portia's phases are full of wordplays and double meanings) 156 **livings**/possessions 150-157 **Though... account**/(this one sentence is notable for its artificiality and increasing hyperbole) 157 **sum**/total and summary 158 **to term**/to speak in terms 161 **she**/(Portia begins to refer to herself in the third person) 167 **converted**/appropriated **But now**/only now 173 **presage**/forecast 174 **vantage**/profit **exclaim on**/protest, lay blame on

Commentary: *The Merchant of Venice* is full of the kind of commercial, contractual language that Portia uses in her monologue. Human beings have a value placed upon them and are subject to accounting procedures. Notice that she loves to give everything at least three values (line 159, 165, 170, 172). When mingled with the fairy tale element in the play (i.e., the gold, silver and lead caskets), the numerical vocabulary takes on a riddling capacity which is also a feature of Portia's speech. Although we are only half way through the play and all seems won by Bassanio, we should remember that this test has only been a ruse, a red herring. The real test lies in the ring: "Let it presage the ruin of your, love,/And be my vantage to exclaim on you." Although she is a favorite Shakespeare heroine, there is a manipulative and cool side to Portia. She loves to play at games, tricks and disguising herself. Even her highly artificial use of language here is a kind of guise. Is she in love with Bassanio or in love with the game of winning and losing? Portia is like Shylock in more ways than we at first imagine. The ring is her bond for a pound of flesh. In her way, she now "owns" Bassanio.

THE MERCHANT OF VENICE

Portia

Act 4, Scene 1. Venice. The Court of Justice. Portia appears at the trial of Shylock vs. Antonio disguised as the learned young lawyer Balthasar. Shylock has been unyielding in recovering his bond: a pound of Antonio's flesh. Here Portia pleads with Shylock to show mercy.

[PORTIA Do you confess the bond?
ANTONIO I do
    PORTIA   Then must the Jew be merciful.
SHYLOCK On what compulsion must I? Tell me that.]
PORTIA
    The quality° of mercy is not strained.°
    It droppeth as the gentle rain from heaven
185 Upon the place beneath. It is twice blest:
    It blesseth him that gives, and him that takes.
    'Tis mightiest in the mightiest. It becomes°
    The thronèd monarch better than his crown.
    His sceptre shows the force of temporal power,
190 The attribute to° awe and majesty,
    Wherein doth sit the dread and fear of kings;
    But mercy is above this sceptred sway.°
    It is enthronèd in the hearts of kings;
    It is an attribute to God himself,
195 And earthly power doth then show likest God's
    When mercy seasons° justice. Therefore, Jew,
    Though justice be thy plea, consider this:
    That in the course of justice none of us
    Should see salvation.° We do pray for mercy,
200 And that same prayer doth teach us all to render°
    The deeds of mercy. I have spoke thus much
    To mitigate° the justice of thy plea,

Which if thou follow, this strict court of Venice
Must needs give sentence 'gainst the merchant
    there.°

183 **quality**/character, nature, function   **strained**/constrained   187
becomes/befits, adorns 190 **attribute to**/visible proof of 192 **sway**/power
of rule 196 **seasons**/moderates, enhances 198-199 **That...salvation**/i.e.,
pure justice, without mercy, would condemn us all because of original sin
200 **render**/return 202 **mitigate**/soften 204 **merchant there**/Antonio

Commentary: Portia's monologue is one of the great set speeches
in Shakespeare.   Mercy is above the law and all else: "'Tis
mightiest in the mightiest." Up until this point, Portia has never
spoken with this kind of nobility and emotion. One wonders if the
costume and mask she adopts allows her the freedom to speak this
way. She has been heralded as a brilliant young doctor of law, so
her speech naturally adopts a kind of brilliance.   But it is so
perfectly set and measured that its lines were almost calculated and
destined to become clichés. The performer must decide how much of
this is an act; a performance of a brilliant speech. But there is
another side to this as well. For the first time in the play, Portia
has been given an important role. She transforms from a bored, rich
heiress into a passionate advocate. She saves a life rather than
money. The speech itself deletes all the profit and loss images that
have riddled most other monologues in the play. On this level, its
honesty and strength is unimpeachable. Yet when Shylock fails to
show mercy, Portia is not above bringing down the wrath of rational
law and exactitude. She will challenge him to cut off exactly one
pound of flesh—no more, no less.

THE MERRY WIVES OF WINDSOR

Mistress Page

Act 2, Scene 1. Town of Windsor. Before Master Page's house. Mistress Page has received a love letter from Falstaff. He hopes to seduce her and get some of her husband's money. She reads the contents of the letter.

MISTRESS PAGE What, have I scaped° love-letters in
    the holiday time° of my beauty, and am I now a
    subject for them? Let me see.
    (She reads)
    "Ask me no reason why I love you, for though
5   Love use Reason for his precision,° he admits him
    not for his counsellor. You are not young; no more
    am I. Go to, then, there's sympathy.° You are
    merry;° so am I. Ha, ha, then, there's more
    sympathy. You love sack,° and so do I. Would you
10   desire better sympathy?° Let it suffice thee, Mistress
    Page, at the least if the love of soldier can suffice,
    that I love thee. I will not say 'pity me'—'tis not a
    soldier-like phrase—but I say 'love me'...
           By me, thine own true knight,
15   By day or night
           Or any kind of light,
           With all his might
           For thee to fight,
              John Falstaff."
    What a Herod of Jewry° is this! O, wicked, wicked
20   world! One that is well-nigh° worn to pieces with
    age, to show himself a young gallant! What an
    unweighed° behavior hath this Flemish° drunkard
    picked, i'th' devil's name, out of my conversation,°
    that he dares in this manner assay° me? Why, he

25   hath not been thrice in my company. What should
      I say to him? I was then frugal of my mirth,
      heaven forgive me. Why, I'll exhibit° a bill in the
      Parliament for the putting down° of men. O God,
      that I knew how to be revenged on him! For
30   revenged I will be, as sure as his guts are made of
      puddings.°

1 scaped/escaped 2 holiday time/i.e., youth 5 precision/i.e., to make its
meaning known 7 sympathy/congeniality 8 merry/fun loving 9 sack/
Spanish wine 10 sympathy/affinity (perhaps an off-color meaning as well)
19 Herod of Jewry/the ranting villain in a mystery play 20 well-nigh/
almost   22 unweighed/ill-considered   Flemish/i.e., the Flemish were
noted for ruddy cheeks from drink 23 conversation/behavior 24 assay/
test 27 exhibit/submit 28 putting down/suppressing   30 guts...
puddings/i.e., sausages

Commentary: Mistress Page's reaction to Falstaff's silly letter is
a mixture of shock and flattery. She says at the beginning that she
has never received love letters. The actor's reaction to the letter
creates the comedy in the scene. So interpretation of the contents
and how these are delivered to the audience is essential. Mistress
Page is of solid, middle-class stock. She is a suburban lady tickled
by the "wicked" mischief of Falstaff. Her speech is full of mild but
colorful oaths. Imbedded in her reaction is the recognition that her
and Falstaff's age put them beyond this kind of dalliance. Her
revenge will be comic, especially when she compares notes with
Mistress Ford who has also received a letter. That scene
immediately follow this.

A MIDSUMMER NIGHT'S DREAM

Helena

Act 1, Scene 1. Athens. The palace of Theseus. Helena is in love with Demetrius who, in turn, loves Helena's more attractive friend, Hermia. Hermia and her lover, Lysander, are planning to elope. She tells Helena of her plans to leave, hoping that her departure will turn Demetrius' affections to Helena. Helena laments on the confusion of love misplaced.

HELENA

How happy some o'er other some° can be!
Through Athens I am thought as fair as she.
But what of that? Demetrius thinks not so.
He will not know what all but he do know.
230 And as he errs,° doting on Hermia's eyes,
So I, admiring of° his qualities.
Things base and vile, holding no quantity,°
Love can transpose° to form and dignity.°
Love looks not with the eyes, but with the mind,
235 And therefore is winged Cupid painted blind.
Nor hath love's mind of any judgement taste;°
Wings and no eyes figure° unheedy haste.
And therefore is love said to be a child
Because in choice he is so oft beguiled.
240 As waggish boys in game° themselves forswear,
So the boy Love° is perjured everywhere.
For ere Demetrius looked on Hermia's eyne°
He hailed down oaths that he was only mine,
And when this hail° some heat from Hermia felt,
245 So he dissolved, and showers of oaths did melt.
I will go tell him of fair Hermia's flight.
Then to the wood will he tomorrow night
Pursue her, and for this intelligence°

If I have thanks it is a dear expense.
250 But herein mean I to enrich my pain,
To have his sight° thither and back again.

226 **some o'er other some**/some in comparison to others   230 **errs**/
mistakes   231 **admiring of**/wondering at   232 **quantity**/proportion   233
transpose/transform   **dignity**/worth   236 **taste**/experience, proof   237
figure/symbolize   240 **game**/sport, fun   241 **boy** Love/Cupid   242 **eyne**/
eyes   244 **hail** (note the sound string with "heat" and "Hermia"; she also
places emphasis on "he" and "her")   248 **intelligence**/information   251
sight/ looks in her direction

Commentary: After having just seen and heard of the strong
mutual bond between Hermia and Lysander, Helena delivers this
soliloquy of romantic woe. Of all the four young lovers, Helena has
the most character. She feels and experiences jealousy and grief. In
fact, her speech is motivated by pain (line 250). Shakespeare tells
us that she is tall and blond. And the actor should note that Helena
suffers from her physical awkwardness. (Attractive and quick,
Hermia, on the other hand, is short and dark.) Whenever Helena
speaks, there is a sense of defeat in whatever she says. Notice the
number of negatives in her lines. The rhyming couplets in her verse
have a number of effects: containing her woe in well measured
portions, demonstrating a child-like relish for pouting, and invest-
ing Helena with a lyrical stoicism that gives her more of a sense of
reality. In the wood *she* will be transformed into the object of the
mens' affections. So for the moment, at least, this is just a self-
indulgence that comes of being the least loved. Later her timidity is
replaced by rage.

A MIDSUMMER NIGHT'S DREAM

Titania

Act 2, Scene 1. The wood near Athens at night. The King and Queen of the Fairies, Oberon and Titania, are quarreling over possession of "a little changeling boy." Each wants the child for their page. Titania tells Oberon of the damage wrought by their arguing.

TITANIA

These are the forgeries° of jealousy,
And never since the middle summer's spring
Met we on hill, in dale, forest, or mead,
By pavèd fountain or by rushy brook,
85 Or in the beachèd margin° of the sea
To dance our ringlets° to the whistling wind,
But with thy brawls° thou hast disturbed our sport.
Therefore the winds, piping to us in vain,
As in revenge have sucked up from the sea
90 Contagious° fogs which, falling in the land,
Hath every pelting river made so proud
That they have overborne their continents.
The ox hath therefore stretched° his yoke in vain,
The ploughman lost his sweat, and the green corn
95 Hath rotted ere his youth attained a beard.
The fold° stands empty in the drownèd field,
And crows are fatted with the murrain flock.°
The nine men's morris° is filled up with mud,
And the quaint mazes° in the wanton° green
100 For lack of tread° are undistinguishable.
The human mortals want their winter cheer.
No night is now with hymn or carol blessed.
Therefore the moon, the governess of floods,
Pale in her anger washes all the air,
105 That rheumatic° diseases do abound;

And thorough° this distemperature we see
The seasons alter: hoary°-headed frosts
Fall in the fresh lap of the crimson rose,
And on old Hiems'° thin and icy crown
110 An odorous chaplet° of sweet summer buds
Is, as in mock'ry, set. The spring, the summer,
The childing autumn, angry winter change
Their wonted liveries, and the mazèd° world
By their increase now knows not which is which;
115 And this same progeny° of evils comes
From our debate, from our dissension.
We are their parents and original.°

81 forgeries/fabrications 85 beached margin/where the waves break on the shore 86 ringlets/fairy circles 87 brawls/quarrels 90 Contagious/noxious 93 stretched/strained 96 fold/enclosure for sheep 97 murrain flock/sheep plagued with disease 98 nine men's morris/open air field games marked out in squares 99 mazes/paths wanton/luxuriant 100 tread/beaten with walking 105 rheumatic/morbid defluxion of humors 106 thorough/through 107 hoary/moldy, white 109 Hiem/personification of winter 110 chaplet/wreath 113 mazed/bewildered 115 progeny/stock 117 original/origin

Commentary: Titania's monologue is one of Shakespeare's most stunning descriptions of the consequences of jealousy. Her images stand apart from the ones used by mortal lovers to describe their emotions; they are on the cosmic level. All of nature is alive and personified. We have to wait until *King Lear* and *The Tempest* before Shakespeare makes such stormy language actualized in physical events on stage. As a character from the natural world, it is only appropriate that Titania should speak in such seasonal images. In the writing, too, there is also the conscious use of language drawn from the quarreling gods of mythology. In that sense, the speech seems more rhetorical than emotional. The actor playing Titania must invest the speech with a greater sense of emotional depth to counteract the unemotional regularity of the verse. Since it is a fairly long speech, it can grow dull rather quickly.

A MIDSUMMER NIGHT'S DREAM

Helena

Act 3, Scene 2. The wood near Athens at night. The mischievous Puck has dropped some magic potion into the eyes of Demetrius and Lysander, causing both to instantly fall in love with Helena. They were previously chasing her friend Hermia. Helena responds to this new confusion, thinking it a cruel trick.

HELENA *(aside)*

Lo, she is one of this confederacy.°
Now I perceive they have conjoined all three
To fashion this false sport in spite of me.—°
195 Injurious° Hermia, most ungrateful maid,
Have you conspired, have you with these contrived
To bait me with this foul derision?
Is all the counsel that we two have shared—
The sisters' vows, the hours that we have spent
200 When we have chid° the hasty-footed time
For parting us—O, is all quite forgot?
All schooldays' friendship, childhood innocence?
We, Hermia, like two artificial° gods
Have with our needles created both one flower,
205 Both on one sampler, sitting on one cushion,
Both warbling of one song, both in one key,
As if our hands, our sides, voices, and minds
Had been incorporate. So we grew together,
Like to a double cherry: seeming parted,
210 But yet an union in partition,
Two lovely berries molded on one stem.
So, with two seeming bodies but one heart,
Two of the first—like coats in heraldry,
Due but to one and crownèd with one crest.
215 And will you rend° our ancient love asunder,

To join with men in scorning your poor friend?
It is not friendly, 'tis not maidenly.
Our sex as well as I may chide you for it,
Though I alone do feel the injury.

[HERMIA
220 I am amazèd at your passionate words.
I scorn you not. It seems that you scorn me.]

HELENA
Have you not set Lysander, as in scorn,
To follow me, and praise my eyes and face?
And made your other love, Demetrius—°
225 Who even but now did spurn° me with his foot—
To call me goddess, nymph, divine, and rare,
Precious, celestial? Wherefore speaks he this
To her he hates? And wherefore doth Lysander
Deny your love so rich within his soul,
230 And tender me, forsooth, affection,
But by your setting on, by your consent?
What though I be not so in grace° as you,
So hung upon with love, so fortunate,
But miserable most, to love unloved—
235 This you should pity rather than despise.

[HERMIA
I understand not what you mean by this.]

HELENA
Ay, do. Persever,° counterfeit sad looks,
Make mouths upon me when I turn my back,
Wink each at other, hold the sweet jest up.
240 This sport well carried shall be chronicled.
If you have any pity, grace, or manners,
You would not make me such an argument.°
But fare ye well. 'Tis partly my own fault,
Which death or absence soon shall remedy.

192 **confederacy**/union, plot (note the cluster of like prefixed words:
"conjoined," "conspired" and "contrived") 194 **in spite of**/to vex 195
Injurious/insulting 200 **chid**/scolded 203 **artificial**/skillful 215 **rend**/

split, tear 224 **Demetrius**/(the actual object of Helen's love, is given added pondering here) 225 **spurn**/i.e., kick 232 **grace**/favor 237 **Persever**/ persevere, persist 242 **argument**/subject for jesting

Commentary: Helena's monologue begins as an extended aside and then becomes a direct address to Hermia. Up until this point, Helena has been suffering in passive woe. Here she is overcome with rage and vents it on Hermia, who is taken aback by the passion of Helena's anger (lines 220-221). Helena, finding no other way to explain the turn around in romantic affection towards her, finds motivation in thinking it a conspiracy. And her speech displays all the residue of paranoia. Imbedded in the lines is the greater fear that a close bosom friendship has been severed (lines 199-216). Part of Puck's prank has been to create the kind of confusion in which a character's inner fears will manifest themselves openly, as they do here. The speech ends with a suggestion of suicide.

OTHELLO

Emilia

Act 4, Scene 3.   Cyprus.   Desdemona's bedroom.
Desdemona is preparing for bed with the help of her
maid, Emilia, who is also Iago's wife.   In this private
moment between the two women, Emilia comments
on the way women are mistreated by men.

[DESDEMONA
  I do not think there is any such woman.
EMILIA
  Yes, a dozen, and as many
  To th' vantage as would store the world they played
    for.
85 But I do think it is their husbands' faults
  If wives do fall. Say that they slack their duties,
  And pour our treasures into foreign laps,°
  Or else break out in peevish° jealousies,
  Throwing restraint upon us; or say they strike us,
90 Or scant our former having in despite:°
  Why, we have galls;° and though we have some
    grace,
  Yet have we some revenge. Let husbands know
  Their wives have sense° like them. They see, and
    smell,
  And have their palates both for sweet and sour,
95 As husbands have. What is it that they do
  When they change° us for others? Is it sport?
  I think it is. And doth affection breed it?
  I think it doth. Is't frailty that thus errs?
  It is so, too. And have not we affections,°
100 Desires for sport, and frailty, as men have?
  Then let them use us well, else let them know
  The ills we do, their ills instruct us so.

87 foreign laps/i.e., other women 88 **peevish**/childish 90 **scant...**
despite/reduce our allowance in spite 91 **galls**/tempers 93 **sense**/feeling
and sexual desire 96 **change**/exchange 99 **affections**/passions,
inclinations

Commentary: Emilia is one of the few honest characters in
Othello. So when she speaks, we listen to the truthfulness of what
she has to say. In sharp contrast to her husband Iago, Emilia is
without spite and jealousy. Although her monologue suggests that
she has been the object of scorn and jealousy, even blows from Iago, it
is not quite a revenge speech, but only implies revenge. Within the
privacy of the moment, Emilia can idealize equality between the
sexes. The speech is a marvelous example of the way a small
monologue can demonstrate a closely etched sense of character.
Emilia's common sense comes, we can't help but think, from having
endured a monster like Iago. The domestic circumstances—Emilia is
preparing Desdemona for bed—adds action to the speech.

PERICLES

Marina

*Act 4, Scene 6. Mytilene. A brothel. Marina, daughter
of Pericles and Thaisa, has been separated from her
parents since birth. Through a series of escapes and
misfortunes, she is discovered in a brothel where she
has been sold to the keeper. Yet her innocence is intact,
as this monologue testifies. She speaks to Lysimachus,
Governor of Mytilene.*

MARINA

Let not authority, which teaches you
To govern others, be the means to make you
100 Misgovern much yourself.
If you were born to honor, show it now;
If put upon you, make the judgement good
That thought you worthy of it. What reason's in
Your justice, who hath power over all,
105 To undo any? If you take from me
Mine honor, you're like him that makes a gap
Into forbidden° ground, whom after
Too many enter, and of all their evils
Yourself are guilty. My life is yet unspotted;°
110 My chastity unstainèd ev'n in thought.
Then if your violence deface this building,
The workmanship of heav'n, you do kill your
   honor,
Abuse your justice, and impoverish me.
My yet good lord, if there be fire before me,
115 Must I straight fly and burn myself? Suppose this
   house°—
Which too too many feel such houses are—
Should be the doctor's patrimony,° and
The surgeon's feeding;° follows it, that I

Must needs infect myself to give them
   maint'nance?
[LYSIMACHUS
   How's this, how's this? Some more. Be sage.]
MARINA *(kneeling)*
120   For me
That am a maid, though most ungentle fortune
Have franked° me in this sty, where since I came
Diseases have been sold dearer° than physic°—
That the gods would set me free from this
   unhallowed place,
125 Though they did change me to the meanest° bird
That flies i'th' purer air!

107 **forbidden**/consecrated, unlawful (The sexual allusions throughout are
probably unintended by the character.) 109 **unspotted**/unstained by sin
115 **house**/charnel house, brothel 117 **patrimony**/heritage 118 **feeding**/
food; i.e., charnel house where disease grows 122 **franked**/enclosed 123
dearer/more richly **physic**/health 125 **meanest**/lowest form of

Commentary: As a character, Marina does not really come to life
until Act 4. *Pericles* is full of such dramatic oddities. As this speech
suggests, Marina is the very soul of innocence. She has preserved
her goodness through all manner of trials. In this scene, she reforms
the lusts of those who frequent the brothel, including Lysimachus,
Governor of Mytilene. So fierce is her chastity, one can detect a
violent tone in Marina's speech: she alternates killing and
infectious images. She is described in the play as "a piece of
virtue." Indeed, she is all of one type and dimension. Her purity
has a kind of purging function. Notice that she likes to wear down
her listeners with a litany of her honor. She uses this kind of
device several times in the play. So ardent is her sense of reform
and virtue that she displays what might be termed a neurotic case
of moral sanitariness.

RICHARD III

Lady Anne

Act 1, Scene 2. London. A street. Lady Anne enters as the only mourner attending the funeral procession of King Henry VI, the last of the Lancaster rulers who has been replaced by the Yorkist Edward IV. Lady Anne's grief and hate are directed at the murderer, Richard of Gloucester.

LADY ANNE

Set down, set down your honorable load,
If honor may be shrouded in a hearse,°
Whilst I a while obsequiously° lament
Th'untimely fall of virtuous Lancaster.°
(They set the coffin down)
5 Poor key-cold° figure of a holy king,
Pale ashes of the house of Lancaster,
Thou bloodless remnant of that royal blood:
Be it lawful that I invocate thy ghost
To hear the lamentations of poor Anne,
10 Wife to thy Edward, to thy slaughtered son,
Stabbed by the selfsame hand° that made these
    wounds.
Lo, in these windows° that let forth thy life,
I pour the helpless° balm of my poor eyes.
O cursèd be the hand that made these holes,
15 Cursèd the blood that let this blood from hence,
Cursèd the heart that had the heart to do it.
More direful hap betide° that hated wretch
That makes us wretched by the death of thee
Than I can wish to wolves, to spiders, toads,
20 Or any creeping venomed thing that lives.
If ever he have child, abortive° be it,
Prodigious,° and untimely brought to light,

Whose ugly and unnatural aspect
May fright the hopeful mother at the view,
25 And that be heir to his unhappiness.°
If ever he have wife, let her be made
More miserable by the death of him
Than I am made by my young lord and thee.—
Come now towards Chertsey° with your holy load,
30 Taken from Paul's to be interrèd there,
(The gentlemen lift the coffin)
And still as° you are weary of this weight°
Rest you, whiles I lament King Henry's corpse.

2 **hearse**/coffin on a bier 3 **obsequiously**//dutifully, mournfully 4 **Lancaster**/i.e., Henry VI, the subject of three previous plays 5 **key-cold**/stone cold 11 **selfsame hand**/i.e., Richard of Gloucester 12 **windows**/eyes 13 **helpless**/useless 17 **hap betide**/fortune befall 21 **abortive**/untimely or monstrous birth (ironic comment on the unnatural birth of Richard) 22 **Prodigious**/monstrous 25 **unhappiness**/evil nature 29 **Chertsey**/monastery near London 31 **still as**/whenever **weary of this weight**/(gives the actor a motive as to why the funeral procession stopped in the first place)

Commentary: Lady Anne's soliloquy is a lament. Not only is it directed towards the dead King, but also towards the whole House of Lancaster. A principal function of the speech is to allow Anne the opportunity to voice curses that, ironically, are aptly descriptive of Richard of Gloucester, the hunchback cripple whose taste for slaughter will help make him King Richard III. Part of the ironic set-up in Lady Anne's speech is the fact that the villainous Richard is waiting in the wings to woo her. All of her venom and curses will be reversed and retracted before the scene ends. Anne's verse is fairly straight-forward and rhetorical. Its main effect is to set a defensive mood that Richard can puncture with his deceit. After marrying Richard, Anne will later die and become a ghostly presence, uttering more curses.

RICHARD III

Lady Anne

Act 1, Scene 2. London. A street. Like a fiend from hell, Richard of Gloucester appears and blocks the funeral procession that is carrying the body of Henry VI to burial. Lady Anne reacts violently and Richard begins, surprisingly, to woo her. He has murdered both her husband and the former King.

LADY ANNE *(to gentlemen and halberdiers)*
    What, do you tremble? Are you all afraid?
    Alas, I blame you not, for you are mortal,
45 And mortal eyes cannot endure the devil.—
    Avaunt,° thou dreadful minister of hell.
    Thou hadst but power over his mortal body;
    His soul thou canst not have; therefore be gone.
[RICHARD GLOUCESTER
    Sweet saint, for charity be not so cursed.°]
LADY ANNE
50 Foul devil, for God's sake hence and trouble us not,
    For thou hast made the happy earth thy hell,
    Filled it with cursing cries and deep exclaims.°
    If thou delight to view thy heinous deeds,
    Behold this pattern° of thy butcheries.—
55 O gentlemen, see, see! Dead Henry's wounds
    Ope their congealèd mouths and bleed afresh!—°
    Blush, blush, thou lump of foul deformity,
    For 'tis thy presence that ex-hales° this blood
    From cold and empty veins where no blood dwells.
60 Thy deed, inhuman and unnatural,
    Provokes this deluge supernatural.
    O God, which this blood mad'st, revenge his death!
    O earth, which this blood drink'st, revenge his
        death!

Either heav'n with lightning strike the murd'rer
   dead,
65 Or earth gape open wide and eat him quick°
   As thou dost swallow up this good king's blood,
   Which his hell-governed arm hath butcherèd!

46 **Avaunt**/be gone 49 **cursed**/sharp-tongued 52 **exclaims**/outcries, accusations 54 **pattern**/example 55-56 **O...afresh!**/(it was believed that the wounds of the murdered would bleed afresh in the presence of the murderer) 58 **ex-hales**/causes to flow 65 **quick**/alive

Commentary: All of Richard's unsettling power and villainy registers in Lady Anne's reaction to him. Notice that her speech is like a protective exorcism. The scene being played is that the devil has come to seize the dead body and Anne, the angel, must protect it. She puts up a barrier of words full of protestations and pleas. The repetition of words like "blood" and "butcheries" gives a lustful quality to her revenges. The verse is laden with vowel sounds that get caught in the back of the throat, mingling there, perhaps, with Lady Anne's sobs. In fact the focus on the mouth (line 56) and words like "drink'st" (line 63), "eat" (line 65) and "swallow" (line 66) gives the speech a taste of vampirism that increases its horror. Once again, Lady Anne's provocative words are meant to show Richard's villainy in high relief.

RICHARD III

Queen Margaret

Act 4, Scene 4. London. Before the palace. Queen Margaret, the widow of Henry VI and now reduced to a witch-like hag, encounters her rival Queen Elizabeth, widow of the slain King Edward IV. Although enemies, both are united in their hatred of Richard III, who has just killed Elizabeth's two young sons in the Tower of London. Margaret mocks Elizabeth.

[QUEEN ELIZABETH
    O thou didst prophesy the time would come
80 That I should wish for thee to help me curse
    That bottled spider, that foul hunch-backed toad.°]
QUEEN MARGARET
    I called thee then "vain° flourish of my fortune;"
    I called thee then, poor shadow, "painted queen,"°
    The presentation of but° what I was,
85 The flattering index° of a direful pageant,°
    One heaved a-high to be hurled down below,°
    A mother only mocked with two fair babes,
    A dream of what thou wast, a garish flag°
    To be the aim of every dangerous shot,
90 A sign° of dignity, a breath, a bubble,
    A queen in jest, only to fill the scene.°
    Where is thy husband now? Where be thy
      brothers?
    Where are thy two sons? Wherein dost thou joy?
    Who sues, and kneels, and says "God save the
      Queen?"
95 Where be the bending° peers that flattered thee?
    Where be the thronging troops that followed thee?
    Decline° all this, and see what now thou art:
    For happy wife, a most distressèd widow;

For joyful mother, one that wails the name;
100 For queen, a very caitiff,° crowned with care;
For one being sued to, one that humbly sues;
For she that scorned at me, now scorned of me;
For she being feared of all, now fearing one;
For she commanding all, obeyed of none.
105 Thus hath the course of justice whirled about,
And left thee but a very prey to time,
Having no more but thought° of what thou wert
To torture thee the more, being what thou art.
Thou didst usurp° my place, and dost thou not
110 Usurp the just proportion of my sorrow?
Now thy proud neck bears half my burdened
    yoke—
From which, even here, I slip my weary head,
And leave the burden of it all on thee.
Farewell, York's wife, and queen of sad mischance.°
115 These English woes shall make me smile in France.
[QUEEN ELIZABETH (*rising*)
O thou, well skilled in curses, stay a while
And teach me how to curse mine enemies.]
QUEEN MARGARET
Forbear° to sleep the nights, and fast the days;
Compare dead happiness with living woe;
120 Think that thy babes were sweeter than they were,
And he that slew them fouler than he is.
Bett'ring° thy loss makes the bad causer worse.
Revolving° this will teach thee how to curse.

81 **That...toad**/refers to the deformed, hunchbacked Richard III 82 **vain**/
foolish 83 **painted queen**/fake queen (also lewd allusion to *strumpet*) 84
presentation of but/only an image 85 **flattering index**/deceptive
prologue **pageant**/show, play 86 **heaved...below**/(a good example of the
contrasting antitheses that fill the speech) 88 **garish flag**/gaudy target 90
sign/token 91 **scene**/(Margaret constantly draws her images from the
theatre) 95 **bending**/bowing 97 **Decline**/recite 100 **caitiff**/wretch 107
thought/memory 109 **usurp**/unjustly assume (one whole question in the
history plays is that of usurpation) 114 **mischance**/fortune 118 **Forbear**/
avoid 122 **Bett'ring**/magnifying 123 **Revolving**/considering, meditating
on

Commentary: The verse of Margaret's lamenting monologue is characterized by the parallel sentences that strengthen the speech with repetitious constructions (lines 91-104). Margaret's words have a tortuous cadence. As Elizabeth says, Margaret is "well skilled in curses." She is the very personification of vengeance and her function throughout *Richard III* is that of a choric figure who speaks horrible prophecies. Often she is played as a mad woman. Part of her motivation here comes from being consumed by rivalry and jealousy. Once a character has fallen from power in Shakespeare, but not to their death, they live the kind of fearsome, twilight existence that Margaret now inhabits. Her language is the language of retribution and witchcraft, filled with antithetical images of foul and fair. Passing on the burden of grief and sorrow is another function of the speech.

ROMEO AND JULIET

Nurse

Act 1, Scene 3. Verona. The Capulet's house. Lady Capulet, the Nurse and Juliet are gathered together for a domestic scene. Juliet is ripe for marriage. This is the first entrance of the two latter characters. The Nurse commands the opening moments of the scene with this monologue full of memories.

NURSE
Faith, I can tell her age unto an hour.
[CAPULET'S WIFE She's not fourteen.]
NURSE I'll lay fourteen of my teeth—and yet, to
15 my teen be it spoken, I have but four—she's not
fourteen. How long is it now to Lammastide?
[CAPULET'S WIFE A fortnight and odd days.]
NURSE
Even or odd, of all days in the year
Come Lammas Eve° at night shall she be fourteen.
20 Susan° and she—God rest all Christian souls!—
Were of an age.° Well, Susan is with God;
She was too good for me.° But, as I said,
On Lammas Eve at night shall she be fourteen,
That shall she, marry, I remember it well.
25 'Tis since the earthquake° now eleven years,
And she was weaned—I never shall forget it—
Of all the days of the year upon that day,
For I had then laid wormwood° to my dug,°
Sitting in the sun under the dovehouse wall.
30 My lord and you were then at Mantua.
Nay, I do bear a brain!° But, as I said,
When it° did taste the wormwood on the nipple
Of my dug and felt it bitter, pretty fool,
To see it tetchy° and fall out wi'th' dug!

128

35   "Shake," quoth the dove-house!° 'Twas no need, I
         trow,
       To bid me trudge;°
       And since that time it is eleven years,
       For then she could stand high-lone.° Nay, by th'
         rood,°
       She could have run and waddled all about,
40   For even the day before, she broke her brow,°
       And then my husband—god be with his soul,
       A was a merry man!—took up the child.
       "Yea," quoth he, "dost thou fall upon thy face?
       Thou wilt fall backward when thou hast more wit,°
45   Wilt thou not, Jule?" And, by my holidam,°
       The pretty wretch left crying and said "Ay."
       To see now how a jest shall come about!°
       I warrant an I should live a thousand years
       I never should forget it. "Wilt thou not, Jule?"
         quoth he,
50   And, pretty fool, it stinted° and said "Ay."

19 **Lammas Eve**/August 1, beginning of the harvest festival for ripe corn
(an allusion to Juliet's marriagable age) 20 **Susan**/(i.e., the Nurse's dead
daughter; suggests a dark memory for the character) 21 **Were of an
age**/were the same age 22 **She...me**/(a pause might come at the end of
this line to let the memory settle) 25 **earthquake**/(this allusion has never
been explained, but it adds an unsettling image to the speech) 28
wormwood/bitter and medicinable herb (another unsettling image)
dug/breast nipple, usually of a beast 31 **bear a brain!**/i.e., have a good
memory for such things 32 **it**/i.e., Juliet as infant 34 **tetchy**/irritable 35
Shake...dovehouse!/a picturesque way of saying the birdhouse shook,
presumably from the earthquake) 35-36 **'Twas...trudge**/i.e., I did't have to
think twice about moving (in fear of the earthquake) (Note the effective
use of repetitive sounds with "time" in next line. There is also a long pause
after "trudge," presumably for the laughs that follow a comic line and its
delivery.) 38 **high-lone**/all alone **rood**/cross of Christ 40 **broke her
brow**/fell and cut her forehead 44 **Thou...wit**/(a bawdy reference to
intercourse) 45 **holidam**/holiness 47 **To...about!**/(another bawdy
suggestion) 50 **stinted**/ceased crying

Commentary: The monologue begins with a quibble over Juliet's
age that unleashes the Nurse's memories. The scene develops the
fact that Juliet is to be married to Paris. It is here we discover that
she is fourteen. The nurse is one of the most entertaining characters

in the play. Her earthy colloquialisms and familiarity with Lady Capulet and Juliet give her endearing qualities and a freedom to speak. Her memory for details, especially the death of her husband and her daughter Susan (who was Juliet's age, and foreshadows Juliet's later doom) in lines 18-21, give her speech a naturalness that is removed from most of the rhetoric in the play so far. Notice how the Nurse is given all kinds of verbal ticks (e.g., "I remember it well," "I never shall forget it," "Nay, I do bear a brain") and digressions that heighten her reality as a character. Her words also heighten the domestic intimacy of the scene. The Nurse has a bawdy side, too, uttering off-color remarks ("When it [Juliet] did taste the wormwood on the nipple/Of my dug") and mild oaths ("by th' rood"). One function of the speech is to set Juliet, the child, in relief in the most affectionate manner. Note, too, that along with the death of Susan and a husband another disturbing factor in the speech is the mention of an earthquake (line 24).

ROMEO AND JULIET

Juliet

Act 2, Scene 2. Verona. The Capulet garden at night.
From her balcony, Juliet thinks about Romeo who she
has just met at the masked ball and whose identity she
has discovered. The Montagues and Capulets are bitter
enemies. Juliet and Romeo are innocents in this
family blood-feud. She cannot hear or see Romeo
below.

JULIET Ay me.
[ROMEO *(aside)*
25 She speaks.
      O, speak again, bright angel; for thou art
      As glorious to this night, being o'er my head,
      As is a wingèd messenger of heaven
      Unto the white upturnèd wond'ring eyes
30 Of mortals that fall back to gaze on him
      When he bestrides the lazy-passing clouds
      And sails upon the bosom of the air.]
JULIET *(not knowing Romeo hears her)*
      O Romeo, Romeo, wherefore° art thou Romeo?
      Deny° thy father and refuse° thy name,
35 Or if thou wilt not, be but sworn my love,
      And I'll° no longer be a Capulet.
[ROMEO *(aside)*
      Shall I hear, or shall I speak at this?]
JULIET
      'Tis but thy name that is my enemy.
      Thou art thyself, though not a Montague.
40 What's Montague? It is nor hand, nor foot,
      Nor arm, nor face, nor any other part
      Belonging to a man. O, be some other name!
      What's in a name? That which we call a rose

By any other word would smell as sweet.
45 So Romeo would, were he not Romeo called,
Retain that dear perfection which he owes°
Without that title. Romeo, doff° thy name,
And for° thy name—which is no part of thee—
Take all myself.

33 **wherefore**/why (i.e., why are you called) 34 **Deny**/disown **refuse**/ renounce 36 **I'll**/(shows Juliet's assertion of will and sense of self) 46 **owes**/owns, possesses 47 **doff**/var. of "daft," to cast off, put aside 48 **for**/in exchange for

Commentary: Juliet's famous soliloquy, overheard by Romeo, is the beginning of an extended duologue between the two young lovers. So often has her speech been quoted that it now seems just a mass of clichés. But rather than being a sighing, lumbering, girlish bit of romantic talk, the verse is actually filled with impatience and impetuousness, more in keeping with Juliet's brisk character. "O Romeo, Romeo, wherefore art thou Romeo," is a searching line demanding an answer and not a dreamy one. Our mistaken view of Juliet often comes from a slavish reading of Romeo's angelic portrait (lines 25-32). Yet Juliet's speech is full of practical solutions to the name barrier: refuse and change names. Her entire speech is one of simple and unadorned words and phrases. The image of the rose is as close as she comes to any thought smacking of sentiment. Phrases like "doff thy name" (line 47) have a quickness and willfulness that make the later speeches of Juliet understandable. "Take all myself" is a line that explodes in complete and certain surrender. Only when Romeo makes his presence known in the next lines does Juliet retreat. But the speech establishes her as a girl with a mind of her own; a mind that is already made up and ready to act.

ROMEO AND JULIET

Juliet

Act 2, Scene 2. Verona. The Capulet garden at night.
Juliet stands on her balcony conversing with Romeo.
They are declaring their love for one another, but are
also aware of the dangers and obstacles of their family
feud.

JULIET

85 Thou knowest the mask° of night is on my face,
Else would a maiden blush bepaint my cheek
For that which thou hast heard me speak tonight.
Fain° would I dwell on form,° fain, fain deny
What I have spoke; but farewell, compliment.°
90 Dost thou love me? I know thou wilt say "Ay,"
And I will take thy word. Yet if thou swear'st
Thou mayst prove false. At lovers' perjuries,
They say, Jove° laughs. O gentle Romeo,
If thou dost love, pronounce° it faithfully;
95 Or if thou think'st I am too quickly won,
I'll frown, and be perverse, and say thee nay,
So thou wilt° woo; but else, not for the world.
In truth, fair Montague, I am too fond,°
And therefore thou mayst think my 'haviour
light.°
100 But trust me, gentleman, I'll prove more true
Than those that have more cunning to be strange.°
I should have been more strange, I must confess,
But that thou overheard'st,° ere I was ware,°
My true-love passion. Therefore pardon me,
105 And not impute this yielding to light love,
Which the dark night hath so discoverèd.°

85 mask/cover (also brings back to mind the "masked ball") 88 Fain/gladly
dwell on form/maintain a formal rather than forward behavior 89 com-

133

pliment/etiquette, politeness 93 **Jove**/ruler of the gods, the almighty 94
pronounce/declare 97 **So thou wilt**/in order to have you 98 **fond**/
infatuated, eager 99 **light**/frivolous 101 **strange**/distant, aloof 103 **But
that thou overheard'st**/(see previous speech above, lines 33-49)
ere...ware/before I was aware of your presence 106 **discoverèd**/revealed
(pronounced as four syllables)

Commentary: Juliet's monologue is both coy and brash. She both
blushes and then demands, "Dost thou love me?" Notice the quick
changes of mood in her speech. Her verbs are all in the superlative
degree: "I am too quickly won;" "I am too fond;" "I'll prove more
true." Once again, Juliet demonstrates a complete commitment to
love. Not just to the *ideal* of romance, but to the person of Romeo.
("But trust me, gentleman, I'll prove more true/Than those that
have more cunning to be strange.") There is an honest, unadorned
quality to her verse; it *seems* lightweight, but it is not. All of the
qualifying "buts" and "yets" and commas break up the rapidity of
the verse into small units. That is the major aspect of the monologue
which the actor must keep under control. Note that there is no
pause within the verse for Romeo to inject a reply. It is swiftly said.
Juliet just has so much to declare, that she does it all in one tumble of
words. Her intention is to convince, with ample evidence, of her
love.

ROMEO AND JULIET

Juliet

Act 3, Scene 2. Verona. Capulet's house. Juliet, now secretly married to Romeo, awaits his return. This is their wedding night. But Romeo has been delayed in the street, where a fight has broken out between followers of the Montagues and Capulets. Unbeknownst to Juliet, Romeo has killed her kinsman, Tybalt.

JULIET
 Gallop apace, you fiery-footed steeds,°
 Towards Phoebus'° lodging! Such a waggoner
 As Phaëton° would whip you to the west
 And bring in cloudy night immediately.
5 Spread thy close° curtain, love-performing night,
 That runaways'° eyes may wink,° and Romeo
 Leap to these arms untalked of and unseen.
 Lovers can see to do their amorous rites
 By their own beauties; or, if love be blind,
10 It best agrees with night. Come, civil° night,
 Thou sober-suited matron all in black,
 And learn° me how to lose° a winning match
 Played for a pair of stainless maidenhoods.°
 Hood° my unmanned° blood, bating° in my cheeks,
15 With thy black mantle till strange° love grown bold
 Think true love acted simple modesty.°
 Come, night; come, Romeo; come, thou day in
  night;
 For thou wilt lie upon the wings of night
 Whiter than new snow on a raven's back.
20 Come, gentle night; come, loving, black-browed
  night;
 Give me my Romeo, and when I shall die°
 Take him and cut him out in little stars,

And he will make the face of heaven so fine
That all the world will be in love with night
25 And pay no worship to the garish sun.
O, I have bought the mansion° of a love
But not possessed it,° and though I am sold,
Not yet enjoyed. So tedious is this day
As is the night before some festival
30 To an impatient child that hath new robes
And may not wear them.

1 **steeds**/horses that draw the chariot of the sun god towards nightfall 2 **Phoebus'**/Apollo, the sun god 3 **Phaëton**/the chariot driver son of Apollo who recklessly drove too near the earth and perished (Pronounced as three syllables: "fay'-i-ton") 5 **close**/concealing 6 **runaways'**/fugitives' **wink**/close 10 **civil**/sober, grave 12 **learn**/teach **lose**/surrender 13 **maidenhoods**/two virginities 14 **Hood**/cover **unmanned**/untamed **bating**/panting 15 **strange**/new, unfamiliar 16 **modesty**/chastity 21 **die**/(sexual meaning: to experience an orgasm), also a rhyming pun with "lie" and "night" 26 **mansion**/dwelling, body 27 **possessed it**/(sexual meaning intended along with "enjoyed" in the next line)

Commentary: Juliet's soliloquy is full of eager and impatient imperatives, leading off with "Gallop apace..." Ironically, the urgency in her speech heightens the tension from the previous scene, even though both are completely separate events. But death hovers over this speech as well. The monologue is an apostrophe to the night. The actor can replace the image of the night with that of Romeo in order to give the speech a clearer motive. Notice all the physical possibilities in the verse: "gallop," "whip," "spread," "wink," "leap" and various forms of "come." From the moment that Romeo and Juliet began paddling palms at the masked ball, there has been an overt physicality to their relationship that is captured in the language. Juliet fills the speech with erotic suggestions. A marriage is to be consummated, which is the intention of the monologue. Although it is kept partially hidden, there is sexual longing in all of Juliet's words; a growing sensuality that comes bounding forth now that she is married: in line 21, she suggests literally seeing stars after sex ("die") with Romeo. The marvelous thing about this speech is that it can be delivered in so many different ways: standing, sitting, kneeling, lying on the back.

ROMEO AND JULIET

Juliet

*Act 3, Scene 2. Verona. The Capulet's house. The
Prince of Verona has banished Romeo from the city for
the death of Juliet's kinsman, Tybalt. Romeo's
departure leaves his young wife Juliet grief-stricken
over two losses: Romeo and Tybalt. Juliet speaks to
her Nurse.*

[NURSE
    Will you speak well of him that killed your
        cousin?]
JULIET
    Shall I speak ill of him that is my husband?
    Ah, poor my lord, what tongue shall smooth thy
        name
    When I, thy three-hours wife, have mangled it?
100 But wherefore,° villain, didst thou kill my cousin?
    That villain cousin would have killed my husband.
    Back, foolish tears, back to your native spring!
    Your tributary drops belong to woe,
    Which you, mistaking, offer up to joy.°
105 My husband lives, that Tybalt would have slain;
    And Tybalt's dead, that would have slain my
        husband.
    All this is comfort. Wherefore weep I then?
    Some word there was, worser than Tybalt's death,
    That murdered me. I would forget it fain,°
110 But O, it presses° to my memory
    Like damnèd guilty deeds to sinners' minds!
    "Tybalt is dead, and Romeo banishèd."°
    That "banishèd," that one word "banishèd"
    Hath slain ten thousand Tybalts. Tybalt's death
115 Was woe enough, if it had ended there;

Or, if sour woe delights in fellowship
And needly° will be ranked° with other griefs,
Why followed not, when she said "Tybalt's dead,"
"Thy father," or "thy mother," nay, or both,
120 Which modern° lamentation might have moved?
But with a rearward° following Tybalt's death,
"Romeo is banishèd"—to speak that word
Is father, mother, Tybalt, Romeo, Juliet,
All slain, all dead. "Romeo is banishèd"—
125 There is no end, no limit, measure, bound,
In that word's death. No words can that woe
sound.°
Where is my father and my mother, Nurse?

100 **wherefore**/why (notice that Juliet also used this word in "Romeo, Romeo, wherefore art thou Romeo"; here it has an ironic twist with "villain") 104 **joy**/i.e., joyfulness of Romeo's survival (note the competing antithesis with "woe") 109 **fain**/gladly 110 **presses**/weighs 112 **banishèd**/outlawed (repeated five times with increasing agony; pronounced as three syllables: "ban i' shed") 117 **needly**/necessarily **ranked**/included 120 **modern**/ordinary 121 **rearward**/rear guard 126 **sound**/fathom the depths of

Commentary: Juliet's tears compete with her words for priority. She is so attuned to language and names that words are the prompts that cause her to immediately respond to any given moment. Here she competes with the words, "Tybalt is dead and Romeo is banishèd." The whole speech revolves around these two motives. Notice how she even goes into the drama of that sentence structure. If words could kill, Juliet certainly feels the power of "banished." Even with characters offstage, Juliet can image them in words. Throughout the verse there are interrupted moments when she even fights the very utterances of words (e.g., lines 122 and 124). There is also probably a silence after line 126. This is a difficult speech to act successfully because it calls for such an authentic display of emotion. Inauthenticity will simply dull its effect.

ROMEO AND JULIET

Juliet

Act 4, Scene 3. Verona. Capulet's house. Juliet's parents order her to wed Paris, yet she is secretly married to the banished Romeo. In despair, she seeks the advice of Friar Laurence, who plots a mock suicide for her with the aid of a sleeping potion. This will enable Romeo to secretly return and take her to Mantua. Juliet has just dismissed her nurse and is alone.

JULIET
    Farewell, God knows when we shall meet again.
15 I have a faint° cold fear thrills° through my veins
    That almost freezes up the heat of life.
    I'll call them back again to comfort me.
    Nurse!—What should she do here?
    (She opens curtains, behind which is seen her bed)
    My dismal° scene I needs must act alone.
20 Come, vial.° What if this mixture do not work at
      all?
    Shall I be married° then tomorrow morning?
    No, no, this° shall forbid it. Lie thou there.
    (She lays down a knife)
    What if it be a poison which the friar
    Subtly hath ministered to have me dead,
25 Lest in this marriage he should be dishonored
    Because he married me before to Romeo?
    I fear it is—and yet methinks it should not,
    For he hath still° been tried° a holy man.
    How if, when I am laid into the tomb,
30 I wake before the time that Romeo
    Come to redeem me? There's a fearful point.
    Shall I not then be stifled in the vault,

To whose foul mouth no healthsome air breathes
   in,
And there die strangled ere my Romeo comes?
35 Or, if I live, is it not very like
The horrible conceit° of death and night,
Together with the terror of the place—
As in a vault, an ancient receptacle
Where for this many hundred years the bones
40 Of all my buried ancestors are packed;
Where bloody Tybalt, yet but green° in the earth,
Lies fest'ring in his shroud; where, as they say,
At some hours in the night spirits resort—
Alack, alack, is it not like that I,
45 So early waking—what with loathsome smells,
And shrieks like mandrakes° torn out of the earth,
That living mortals, hearing them, run mad—
O, if I wake, shall I not be distraught,
Environèd° with all these hideous fears,
50 And madly play with my forefathers' joints,°
And pluck the mangled Tybalt from his shroud,
And, in this rage,° with some great° kinsman's
   bone
As with a club dash out my desp'rate brains?
O, look! Methinks I see my cousin's ghost
55 Seeking out Romeo that did spit° his body
Upon a rapier's point. Stay,° Tybalt, stay!
Romeo, Romeo, Romeo! Here's drink. I drink to
   thee.
*(She drinks from the vial and falls upon the bed,
pulling closed the curtains)*

15 faint/fainting thrills/piercing 19 dismal/dreadful 20 vial/i.e., sleeping
potion 21 married/i.e., to Paris 22 this/i.e., the knife 28 still/always
tried/proved 36 conceit/idea 41 green/newly planted 46 mandrakes/a
plant whose forked root resembled human beings and, when pulled from
the ground, was fabled to utter a shriek and cause death or insanity 49
Environèd/surrounded (pronounced as three syllables) 50 joints/bones
52 rage/madness, fit great/earlier relative 55 spit/stab 56 Stay/stop

Commentary: Juliet's soliloquy is full of fears and doubts about the potency of the Friar's plan. She has good reason to feel this way because it will fail. So her speech foreshadows that doom. There is hardly a speech of Juliet's where "night" and "death" have not cast shadows across her words. Notice how conscious Juliet, still a young woman, is of death. A lot of preparation and action is called for. This monologue is full of visions that grow in horror and intensity. The danger for the actor is the possibility of becoming too overwrought too early, since the speech is long and involved before the final decision to drink the potion comes. This is really the moment where Juliet feels the presence of death. The images she calls forth are particularly grotesque (lines 35-53, one complete sentence). Delirium is called for in lines 54-56.

THE TAMING OF THE SHREW

Katherine

Act 5, Scene 2. Padua. Lucentio's house during a wedding feast. Katherine (Kate), after a fiery courtship and sudden marriage, has learned to obey her husband Petruchio. Her shrewish temper, though not completely gone, is now kept under control. Here she tells the wedding assembly about the virtues of conformity and wifely duty.

[PETRUCHIO
Katherine, I charge thee tell these headstrong
women
What duty they do owe their lords and husbands.
WIDOW
Come, come, you're mocking. We will have no
telling.
PETRUCHIO
Come on, I say, and first begin with her.
  WIDOW She shall not.
PETRUCHIO
135 I say she shall: and first begin with her.]
KATHERINE
Fie,° fie, unknit that threat'ning,° unkind brow,
And dart not scornful glances from those eyes
To wound thy lord, thy king, thy governor.
It blots° thy beauty as frosts do bite the meads,°
140 Confounds° thy fame° as whirlwinds shake fair
buds,
And in no sense is meet° or amiable.
A woman moved° is like a fountain troubled,
Muddy, ill-seeming, thick, bereft of beauty,
And while it is so, none so dry or thirsty
Will deign to sip or touch one drop of it.
145 Thy husband is thy lord, thy life, thy keeper,

Thy head, thy sovereign, one that cares for thee,
And for thy maintenance° commits his body
To painful labor both by sea and land,
To watch° the night in storms, the day in cold,
150 Whilst thou liest warm at home, secure and safe,
And craves no other tribute at thy hands
But love, fair looks, and true obedience,
Too little payment for so great a debt.
Such duty as the subject owes the prince,
155 Even such a woman oweth to her husband,
And when she is froward,° peevish, sullen, sour,
And not obedient to his honest will,
What is she but a foul contending° rebel,
And graceless traitor to her loving lord?
160 I am ashamed that women are so simple°
To offer war where they should kneel for peace,
Or seek for rule, supremacy, and sway°
When they are bound to serve, love, and obey.
Why are our bodies soft, and weak, and smooth,
165 Unapt° to toil and trouble in the world,
But that our soft conditions° and our hearts
Should well agree with our external parts?
Come, come, you froward and unable worms,°
My mind hath been as big° as one of yours,
170 My heart as great, my reason haply more,
To bandy word for word and frown for frown;
But now I see our lances are but straws,
Our strength as weak, our weakness past° compare,
That seeming to be most which we indeed least are.
175 Then vail your stomachs, for it is no boot,°
And place your hands below your husband's foot,
In token of which duty, if he please,
My hand is ready, may it do him ease.°

136 **Fie**/(used to express disagreement or shock) **threat'ning**/angry,
warlike (pronounced as two syllables) 139 **blots**/stains, tarnishes **meads**/
meadows 140 **Confounds**/ruins **fame**/reputation 141 **meet**/ proper, fit

143

142 **moved**/made angry 147 **maintenance**/upkeep 149 **To watch**/to keep alert for 156 **froward**/willful, rebellious 158 **contending**/ warlike 160 **simple**/foolish 162 **sway**/control 165 **Unapt**/unfit 166 **conditions**/ qualities 168 **unable worms**/weak, lowly creatures 169 **big**/inflated 173 **past**/beyond 175 **Then...boot**/Then lower your pride, for there is no advantage in it 178 **do him ease**/give him pleasure

Commentary: Kate's final moralizing monologue is about duty and obedience. Just how straight forward or tongue-in-cheek the message is really depends on the actor's interpretation. Kate has been transformed from a wild tempest into a domestic calm, and the change has been a radical one. She submits to Petruchio because of his outrageous treatment of her. But just how convinced is she? The residue of Kate's stormy personality still lives in her verse. Her words are about war and peace. Most of her speech is about different kinds of trials born with difficulty. Kate knows about romantic hell because she has been through it. Throughout the comic action, she has undergone an education in order to find a secure place within an ordered realm: the husband is "prince" and shrewish wife "but a foul contending rebel,/And graceless traitor to her loving lord..." Note, too, how she uses antithesis: ugliness with beauty, hard with soft, cold and warm, hardship and comfort.

THE TEMPEST

Miranda

Act 1, Scene 2. Prospero's Island. In front of Prospero's cell. Miranda has just witnessed the full might of her father Prospero's magic: a storm so violent it has sunk a ship and its crew. Miranda makes this plea to her father. It is her first appearance in the play.

MIRANDA

   If by your art,° my dearest father, you have
   Put the wild waters in this roar,° allay them.
   The sky, it seems, would pour down stinking
      pitch,°
   But that the sea, mounting to th' welkin's° cheek,
5 Dashes the fire out. O, I have sufferèd
   With those that I saw suffer! A brave° vessel,°
   Who had, no doubt, some noble creature in her,
   Dashed all to pieces! O,° the cry did knock
   Against my very heart! Poor souls, they perished.
10 Had I been any god of power, I would
   Have sunk the sea within the earth, or ere°
   It should the good ship so have swallowed and
   The fraughting° souls within her.

1 art/magical powers 2 **wild waters in this roar**/(Note the onomatopoeic sounds of these words and others she speaks.) 3 pitch/black, tar-like substance 4 **welkin's cheek**/sky's face 6 **brave**/fine **vessel**/the ship, but can also mean a body 8 **O**/an expression of grief here and above 11 **or ere**/before 13 **fraughting**/cargoed **souls**/(*souls* completes a string of sounds with the other sibilants above)

Commentary: The image of pure, uncorrupted innocence in *The Tempest*, Miranda really has only this one monologue and her scenes with Ferdinand. Her naiveté, youth and isolation on the island has not given her a strong or rich sense of character. But she does display here an emotion, compassion and glimpse of outrage that certainly surprises Prospero. She is even crying during the speech.

The scene she has witnessed has clearly been a shocking vision; the residue of its turbulence is still in her verse. And she has "suffered" each stage of the tempest and each loss of life. It is interesting to note that the previous scene was a spectacular display of the storm and its effects on the ship's crew. Here Miranda offers a cameo play-back of that larger frame. A "noble" soul herself, Miranda naturally concludes that all souls lost on that ship were noble, too. Much of the play that follows is Prospero's way of educating her more wisely in the real ways of the world. Notice her deep identification with those who've drowned. This is something an actor can isolate and use.

TROILUS AND CRESSIDA

Cressida

Act 1, Scene 2. Troy. Before Priam's palace. Cressida, daughter of the Trojan priest Calchas, is being wooed by the young Trojan prince Troilus through the efforts of a go-between, Pandarus, Cressida's perverse uncle. Cressida speaks after one such wooing scene.

CRESSIDA By the same token, you are a bawd.
   (Exeunt Pandarus)
   Words, vows, gifts, tears, and love's full sacrifice
   He offers in another's enterprise;
280 But more in Troilus thousandfold I see
   Than in the glass of Pandar's praise may be.
   Yet hold I off.° Women are angels, wooing;°
   Things won are done.° Joy's soul lies in the doing.°
   That she° beloved knows naught° that knows not
     this:
285 Men price the thing ungained more than it is.°
   That she was never yet that ever knew
   Love got so sweet as when desire did sue.°
   Therefore this maxim out of love° I teach"
   Achievement is command; ungained, beseech.°
290 Then though my heart's contents firm° love doth
     bear,
   Nothing of that shall from mine eyes appear.°

---

282 **hold I off**/i.e., I must restrain myself **Women...wooing**/i.e., Women are angels to men while being wooed 283 **Things...done**/i.e., once she is won, all the tenderness is over **doing/performance** (also sexual allusion to intercourse) 284 **she**/any woman **naught**/nothing 285 **Men...is**/Men value women as sexual objects more before rather than after 287 **Love... sue**/i.e., Love gotten easily and without yearning desire is not nearly so sweet 288 **out of love**/derived from love's book of rules or for the benefit of love 289 **Achievement...beseech**/i.e., Once a male conquers he is in command; deny him easy access and he will beg 290 **firm**/genuine, certain 291 **appear**/show, be evidenced

Commentary: Although young, Cressida has a knowledge of the world surpassing that of most of the warring lords in the play. She knows love is a commodity. Her speech is direct, calculating and to the point. Yes, Troilus is a man she can love and give herself to (she is "firm" about that), but not in a blind, romantic way. She goes into this affair with eyes open. She can call a bawd a bawd and will switch sides at the slightest hint of dishonesty. She is the hard-edged agent of plain speaking in a play where dishonesty and corruption are just about the only motivations on display. It is typical for Cressida to have such short maxim-like soliloquies. She never reveals too much at a time. The verse is written like brief memorandums; notes that include do's and dont's: "Achievement is command; ungained, beseech." A character who utters maxims all the time is a difficult one to penetrate and play. And Shakespeare has deliberately made Cressida something of an ambiguous cipher. In a play that is like *Romeo and Juliet*, Cressida has little of Juliet's personality and exuberance. She calculates each step before taking the next. Her warmth is matched by coldness. Some in the play, like Ulysses, think she is a manipulating harlot. But then we never really know the true depth of her thoughts.

TROILUS AND CRESSIDA

Cressida

Act 3, Scene 2. Troy. The garden of Calchas. Troilus and Cressida, young lovers in the midst of the protracted Trojan War, meet for the first time in the garden of Cressida's home. The two lovers have been brought together by the unsavory Pandarus.

[TROILUS
    Why was my Cressid then so hard to win?]
CRESSIDA
    Hard to seem° won; but I was won, my lord,
115 With the first glance that ever—pardon me:°
    If I confess much, you will play the tyrant.°
    I love you now, but till now not so much
    But I might master it.° In faith, I lie:°
    My thoughts were like unbridled children, grown
120 Too headstrong for their mother. See, we fools!
    Why have I blabbed? Who shall be true to us,
    When we are so unsecret to ourselves?
    But though I loved you well, I wooed you not—
    And yet, good faith, I wished myself a man,
125 Or that we women had men's privilege
    Of speaking first. Sweet, bid me hold my tongue,°
    For in this rapture° I shall surely speak
    The thing I shall repent. See,° see, your silence,
    Cunning in dumbness, in my weakness draws
130 My soul of counsel from me. Stop my mouth.°

---

114 **seem**/(Cressida gives this word stress to counter Troilus' question. *Seeming* and *being* are two major themes in the play.) 115 **pardon me**/(Cressida pauses with this line in order not to declare her love too openly too soon. A pause is indicated at the dash.) 116 **tyrant**/ruler, have the upper hand 118 **master it**/control it **I lie**/(She changes directions here, with another pause, and makes the choice to reveal her passions.) 126 **hold my tongue**/i.e., I have said too much 127 **rapture**/passion 128

See/(notices the other character's mood) 130 **Stop my mouth**/kiss me, quiet me

Commentary: Cressida explains to Troilus that although it took time for him to win her, it bears no relationship to the value of her love for him. That is genuine. Cressida's impulse from the start of this affair has been to conceal feelings and not appear too hasty. Yet here some of those impulsive convictions are blurted out and supported by words like "unbridled" and "blabbed." Were this *Romeo and Juliet*, the romantic element would be played to the hilt. But in Cressida's verse, love vows peek out from behind the concealments: "Sweet, bid me hold my tongue,/For in this rapture I shall surely speak/The thing I shall repent." Cressida knows there is a political ("cunning") side to new love. What is he after?, she seems to be asking. The actor must remember the affair between Troilus and Cressida develops amidst the war between the Trojans and Greeks. Ruin is certain for the former, and so this love affair carries with it all the foreboding sentiments of doom. Everything about it seems unnatural and calculated. Notice how she can release a bit of passion and then quickly shut the door again.

TWELFTH NIGHT

Viola

Act 2, Scene 2. Illyria. The street outside the Lady Olivia's house. In disguise as the page Cesario, Viola has just left Olivia after delivering a love suit from Duke Orsino. But Olivia's fancy has turned towards "Cesario." Pursued from the house by the steward, Malvolio, Viola has been given a ring from Olivia. Malvolio throws it at her feet when she rejects it.

VIOLA *(picking up the ring)*
    I left no ring with her. What means this lady?
    Fortune forbid my outside have not° charmed her.
    She made good view of me,° indeed so much
20 That sure methought her eyes had lost her
       tongue,°
    For she did speak in starts, distractedly.
    She loves me, sure.° The cunning° of her passion
    Invites me in° this churlish messenger.°
    None of my lord's ring! Why, he sent her none.
25 I am the man.° If it be so—as 'tis°—
    Poor lady, she were better love a dream!
    Disguise, I see thou art a wickedness
    Wherein the pregnant enemy° does much.
    How easy is it for the proper false°
30 In women's waxen° hearts to set their forms!°
    Alas, our frailty° is the cause, not we,
    For such as we are made of, such we be.
    How will this fadge?° My master loves her dearly,
    And I, poor monster,° fond as much on him;
35 And she, mistaken, seems to dote on me.
    What will become of this? As I am man,
    My state is desperate° for my master's love.
    As I am woman, now, alas the day!

What thriftless° sighs shall poor Olivia breathe!
40 O time, thou must untangle this, not I.
    It is too hard a knot for me t'untie.

18 **not**/(in modern English, the "not" is redundant) 19 **made...me**/
examined me closely 20 **her...tongue**/i.e., her steady look made her lose
the power to speak 22 **sure**/i.e., I am convinced **cunning**/craftiness 23
in/by means of **this...messenger**/i.e., Malvolio 25 **I...man**/i.e., who she
loves **'tis**/i.e., it certainly seems 28 **pregnant enemy**/i.e., Satan in disguise
29 **proper false**/falsely attractive 30 **waxen**/impressionable **forms**/
images 31 **frailty**/human weakness 33 **fadge**/turn out 34 **monster**/i.e.,
because she is both "man" and woman 37 **desperate**/hopeless 39
thriftless/unprofitable

Commentary: Viola's soliloquy sums up the romantic complications and irony that pain the principal characters in the play. Here
she suddenly discovers that her disguise is not a source of strength,
but "frailty." As the page "boy" Cesario, Viola must battle her
affections for her master, Duke Orsino, and as a go-between to
Olivia, she suddenly finds herself the object of that lady's
infatuation (noted in lines 18-23). Viola shares her dilemma with
the audience, the only ones to whom she can openly appeal for
understanding. Outwardly she must "play" Cesario, but inwardly
she is Viola and full of female sensibility. This contrast between
appearance and reality, the play's strongest theme, is totally
embodied in Viola/Cesario. The verse of the monologue gives her a
chance to debate this point with herself.

THE TWO GENTLEMEN OF VERONA

Julia

Act 1, Scene 2. Verona. The garden of Julia's house. Julia, the beloved of Proteus, who has several other suitors, receives a love letter from him which she impetuously tears up. But once her maid Lucetta leaves, she lovingly tries to piece the letter back together.

JULIA
This bauble° shall not henceforth trouble me.
100 Here is a coil° with protestation.
(She tears the letter and drops the pieces)
[Go, get you gone, and let the papers lie.
You would be fing'ring them to anger me.
LUCETTA *(aside)*
She makes it strange, but she would be pleased
To be so angered with another letter. *Exit*
JULIA
105 Nay, would I were so angered with the same.]
O hateful hands, to tear such loving words;
Injurious wasps,° to feed on such sweet honey
And kill the bees that yield it with your stings.
I'll kiss each several paper° for amends.
(She picks up some of the pieces of paper)
110 Look, here is writ "Kind Julia"—unkind° Julia,
As in revenge of thy ingratitude
I throw° thy name against the bruising stones,
Trampling° contemptuously on thy disdain.
And here is writ "Love-wounded Proteus."
115 Poor wounded name, my bosom as a bed°
Shall lodge thee till thy wound be throughly°
healed;
And thus I search° it with a sovereign kiss.

153

But twice or thrice was "Proteus" written down.
Be calm, good wind, blow not a word away
120 Till I have found each letter in the letter
Except mine own name. That, some whirlwind
     bear
Unto a ragged, fearful, hanging rock
And throw it thence into the raging sea.
Lo, here in one line is his name twice writ:
125 "Poor forlorn Proteus," "passionate Proteus,"
"To the sweet Julia"—that I'll tear away.
And yet I will not, sith° so prettily
He couples it to his complaining° names.
Thus will I fold them, one upon another.
130 Now kiss, embrace, contend, do what you will.

99 **bauble**/trifle (also appears as "babble") 100 **coil**/fuss, disturbance 107
wasps/i.e., refers to her fingers 109 **several paper**/separate fragments
110 **unkind**/unnatural, cruel 112 **I throw**/(she throws down the piece of
paper on which her name appears) 113 **Trampling**/(she steps on it) 115
my...bed/(she holds the fragment to her bosom) 116 **throughly**/
thoroughly 117 **search**/probe 127 **sith**/since 128 **complaining**/
languishing

Commentary: Julia, as her words and actions indicate, is a willful
and headstrong young woman. She is plagued with indecision about
who or how to love. The whole experience of the emotion is new to
her. But after she has destroyed Proteus' letter, she is instantly on
her knees savoring each fragment. The motivation that spurs Julia
to fall in love with Proteus comes through this kind of effort. The
task of reconstructing the letter is like discovering the meaning of
love in emblematic words and phrases. Few of Shakespeare's
soliloquies are this active and full of possibilities. Notice how she
searches the stage for each scrap until the whole thing is
reassembled into a pile. Yet when her maid returns, she is once more
"lady disdain," turning her back on the heap of words.

THE TWO GENTLEMEN OF VERONA

Julia

Act 4, Scene 4. Milan. Outside the Duke's palace. Julia, in pursuit of her love, Proteus, has secretly followed him to Milan where she has entered his service as the disguised page "Sebastian." But Proteus is now infatuated with Silvia, to whom Sebastian has just delivered the very ring which she, Julia, gave to Proteus on his departure from Verona. Silvia denies the ring after hearing about Julia's grace and devotion from "Sebastian" and departs the stage.

JULIA

    [And she° shall thank you for't, if e'er you know
       her.—
    A virtuous gentlewoman, mild, and beautiful.
    I hope my master's suit will be but cold,°
    Since she respects "my mistress'" love so much.]
180 Alas, how love can trifle with itself.
    Here° is her picture. Let me see, I think
    If I had such a tire,° this face of mine
    Were full as lovely as is this of hers.
    And yet the painter flattered her a little,
185 Unless I flatter with myself too much.
    Her hair is auburn, mine is perfect yellow.
    If that be all the difference in his love,
    I'll get me such a colored periwig.
    Her eyes are grey as glass, and so are mine.
190 Ay, but her forehead's low, and mine's as high.°
    What should it be that he respects° in her
    But I can make respective in myself,
    If this fond love were not a blinded god?
    Come, shadow, come, and take this shadow up,°
    For 'tis thy rival.

(She picks up the portrait)

195   O thou senseless° form,
Thou shalt be worshipped, kissed, loved, and
   adored;
And were there sense° in his idolatry
My substance should be statue in thy stead.
I'll use thee kindly, for thy mistress' sake,
200 That used me so; or else, by Jove I vow,
I should have scratched out your unseeing eyes,
To make my master out of love with thee.

176 **she**/i.e., Julia 178 **cold**/vain 181 **Here**/(discovers Silvia's picture) 182 **tire**/headdress 190 **as high**/i.e., as high as her's is low 191 **respects**/cares for 194 **take...up**/i.e., show up this image with your own 195 **senseless**/insensitive 197 **sense**/reason

Commentary: Just as she acted out her emotions through the torn letter in Act 1, here Julia delivers this soliloquy through the act of comparing herself with Silvia's portrait. Having made a friend of Silvia, the rivalry between the two women is diffused, "Since she [Silvia] respects 'my mistress" [Julia's] love so much." Trapped in a male guise (like Viola in *Twelfth Night*), Julia is at the mercy of her own deceit. She searches the portrait for reasons why Proteus should love Silvia and not she. But love knows no sense and physical form is but a shadow. Julia's fierceness returns in line 201. Although disarmed by Silvia's goodness, a ray of rivalry remains.

THE TWO NOBLE KINSMEN

Jailer's Daughter

Act 2, Scene 4. Athens. The prison. Palamon, a The-
ban, has been imprisoned together with his kinsman
(cousin) Arcite for defending their city against the Duke
of Athens. While in prison, the Jailer's Daughter falls
madly in love with Palamon, creating the basis for a
plot device.

JAILER'S DAUGHTER
    Why should I love this gentleman? 'Tis odds°
    He never will affect° me. I am base,°
    My father the mean° keeper of his prison,
    And he a prince. To marry him is hopeless,
5   To be his whore is witless.° Out upon't,
    What pushes° are we wenches driven to
    When fifteen° once has found us? First, I saw him;
    I, seeing, thought he was a goodly man;
    He has as much to please a woman in him—
10 If he pleases to bestow it so—as ever
    These eyes yet looked on. Next, I pitied him,
    And so would any young wench, o'my conscience,
    That ever dreamed or vowed her maidenhead
    To a young handsome man. Then, I loved him,
15 Extremely loved him, infinitely loved him—
    And yet he had a cousin° fair as he, too.
    But in my heart was Palamon, and there,
    Lord, what a coil he keeps!° To hear him
    Sing in an evening, what a heaven it is!
20 And yet his songs are sad ones. Fairer spoken
    Was never gentleman. When I come in
    To bring him water in a morning, first
    He bows his noble body, then salutes me, thus:°

"Fair, gentle maid, good morrow. May thy
    goodness
25 Get thee a happy husband." Once he kissed me°—
I loved my lips the better ten days after.
Would he would do so every day! He grieves
    much,
And me as much to see his misery.
What should I do to make him know I love him?
30 For I would fain° enjoy him. Say I ventured
To set him free? What says the law then? Thus
    much°
For law or kindred! I will do it,
And this night; ere° tomorrow he shall love me.

1 'Tis odds/odds are 2 affect/love base/of low birth 3 mean/i.e., menial
5 witless/stupid, mad 6 pushes/urges, extremes 7 fifteen/(her age) 16
cousin/Arcite, the other kinsman 18 coil he keeps/i.e., turmoil he makes
23 thus/(Indicates that she acts out the action she describes.) 25 kissed
me/(A pause is indicated after the line to show that the idea registers for
the actor.) 30 would fain/am eager to 31 Thus much/(Indicates some
dismissive action.) 33 ere/before

Commentary: The Jailer's nameless Daughter, although pri-
marily a mechanical device invented to get Palamon out of jail,
takes on rich life as a character. Her entire motivation is focused on
her infatuation with Palamon. And her speeches are filled with
the grief that budding romance brings. She is stricken, at fifteen,
with love at first sight. Notice how she uses all the gush and exag-
geration of any modern teenager: "Then, I loved him,/Extremely
loved him, infinitely loved him..." Ten days after kissing her,
Palamon's lips are still a fresh memory. The speech also represents
a decision making process (lines 29-33). Inherent in the Daughter's
remarks is the full knowledge that her love will never be requited:
"'Tis odds/He never will affect me." Like Ophelia in *Hamlet*, the
Jailer's Daughter must play the part of love's pawn. (Note: It is
generally believed that the playwright John Fletcher wrote this
speech and the scenes in which the Jailer's Daughter appears.)

THE TWO NOBLE KINSMEN

Jailer's Daughter

Act 2, Scene 5.   Athens.   The prison.   The Jailer's Daughter, infatuated with Palamon, has gone to the extreme of releasing him from prison.   Here she reports on the act.

JAILER'S DAUGHTER

    Let all the dukes and all the devils roar—
    He is at liberty!° I have ventured° for him,
    And out I have brought him. To a little wood
    A mile hence I have sent him, where a cedar
5   Higher than all the rest spreads like a plane,
    Fast° by a brook—and there he shall keep close°
    Till I provide him files° and food, for yet
    His iron bracelets are not off. O Love,°
    What a stout-hearted child thou art! My father
10 Durst better have endured° cold iron° than done it.
    I love him beyond love and beyond reason
    Or wit° or safety. I have made him know it—
    I care not, I am desperate. If the law
    Find me,° and then condemn me for't, some
      wenches,
15 Some honest-hearted maids, will sing my dirge
    And tell to memory my death was noble,
    Dying almost a martyr. That way he takes,
    I purpose, is my way too. Sure, he cannot
    Be so unmanly as to leave me here.
20 If he do, maids will not so easily
    Trust men again. And yet, he has not thanked me
    For what I have done—no, not so much as kissed
      me—
    And that, methinks, is not so well. Nor scarcely
    Could I persuade him to become a free man,

25   He made such scruples of the wrong he did
       To me and to my father. Yet, I hope
       When he considers more, this love of mine
       Will take more root within him. Let him do
       What he will with me—so° he use me kindly.°
30   For use me,° so he shall, or I'll proclaim him,°
       And to his face, no man.° I'll presently°
       Provide him necessaries and pack my clothes up,
       And where there is a patch of ground° I'll venture,°
       So° he be with me. By him, like a shadow,
35   I'll ever dwell. Within this hour the hubbub
       Will be all o'er the prison—I am then
       Kissing the man they look for. Farewell, father:
       Get many more such prisoners and such daughters,
       And shortly you may keep yourself.° Now to him.

2 at liberty/free ventured/risked 6 Fast/close keep close/stay in hiding
7 files/i.e., for his chains 8 Love/Cupid 10 Durst...endured/would have
suffered death cold iron/by sword (i.e., beheading) 12 wit/good sense 14
Find me/discover what I have done 29 so/provided that kindly/gently 30
use me/i.e., in a sexual way proclaim him/announce it publicly 31 no
man/i.e., impotent presently/at once 33 patch of ground/path
venture/hazard 34 So/provided that 39 keep yourself/i.e., look after
yourself when all are gone off

Commentary: The Daughter's soliloquy begins in liberation. Not
only has she freed her love, Palamon, but she has freed herself from
her father. In this respect she is much like Jessica, the daughter of
Shylock in *The Merchant of Venice.* The Daughter recognizes how
daring she has been (lines 11-17). Comparing herself to a "martyr,"
she puts herself in the company of all romantic heroines. But then
distrust creeps into her speech. Will Palamon return her love and
sacrifice in kind? Notice how much of the speech is given over to
"he" and "him." The Daughter's selflessness leaves her danger-
ously alone. In each of her speeches there is a sense of foreboding
doom. This is reinforced by the fact that we have yet to see the
Daughter with Palamon, but always by herself. (Note: It is
generally believed that the playwright John Fletcher wrote this
speech and the scenes in which the Jailer's Daughter appears.)

THE WINTER'S TALE

Hermione

Act 3, Scene 2. Sicilia. A Court of Justice. The dignified and perfectly chaste Hermione has been unjustly accused of adultery by her unreasonable husband King Leontes. Brought to trial by him, she pleads her innocence.

[LEONTES   Your actions are my "dreams."
    You had a bastard by Polixenes,
    And I but dreamed it. As you were past all
       shame—
    Those of your fact are so—so past all truth;
85 Which to deny concerns more than avails; for as
    Thy brat hath been cast out, like to itself,
    No father owning it—which is indeed
    More criminal in thee than it—so thou
    Shalt feel our justice, in whose easiest passage
    Look for no less than death.]

HERMIONE
90   Sir, spare your threats.
    The bug° which you would fright me with, I seek.
    To me can life be no commodity.°
    The crown and comfort of my life, your favor,
    I do give° lost, for I do feel it gone
95 But know not how it went. My second joy,°
    And first fruits of my body, from his presence
    I am barred, like one infectious. My third comfort,
    Starred° most unluckily, is from my breast,
    The innocent milk in it° most innocent mouth,
100 Haled° out to murder; myself on every post°
    Proclaimed a strumpet, with immodest hatred
    The childbed privilege denied, which 'longs°
    To women of all fashion;° lastly, hurried

Here, to this place, i'th' open air, before
105 I have got strength of limit.° Now, my liege,
Tell me what blessings I have here alive,
That I should fear to die? Therefore proceed.
But yet hear this—mistake me not—no life,
I prize it not a straw; but for mine honor,
110 Which I would free:° if I shall be condemned
Upon surmises,° all proofs sleeping else
But what your jealousies awake, I tell you
'Tis rigor, and not law.° Your honors all,
I do refer me to the oracle.
Apollo be my judge.

91 **bug**/bogey, fear (i.e., death) 92 **commodity**/asset 94 **give**/reckon as 95 **second joy**/i.e., her son, Mamillius 98 **Starred**/fated 99 **it**/its 100 **Haled**/hailed **post**/i.e., for public notices 102 **'longs**/belongs 103 **fashion**/rank 105 **strength of limit**/i.e., period of rest after recent child-bearing 110 **free**/clear 111 **surmises**/suppositions 113 **rigor, and not law**/tyranny, not justice

Commentary: Hermione's strongest quality is her patience in adversity. The raging Leontes is her opposite in all regards. Just compare his speech with hers. Her verse is dignified, certain and direct. Her monologue is a defense speech. His speech is a rant. She offers each of her joys as a sorrow lost. Hermione has a spotless virtue that is above the human law. In fact, she can really only be judged by Apollo, whose oracle finds her innocent. In her monologue we detect logic and a polished eloquence that is almost emotionless. But when her honor, rather than her person, is under attack, she comes alive in lines 108-114. Her "mistake me not" is as close as Hermione ever comes to delivering a threat.

THE WINTER'S TALE

Paulina

*Act 3, Scene 2. Sicilia. A Court of Justice. Hermione,
wife of the jealous King Leontes, has been unjustly
accused of adultery. An oracle proves her chaste and
true. In the meantime, though, their son Mamillius
has died of grief and the noble woman Paulina enters
to report that Hermione has just died as well. Here she
accuses Leontes of tyranny against his friends, wife and
children.*

PAULINA   Woe the while!
   O cut my lace,° lest my heart, cracking it,
   Break too.
[A LORD   What fit is this, good lady?]
PAULINA *(to Leontes)*
   What studied° torments, tyrant, hast° for me?
175 What wheels, racks, fires? What flaying,° boiling
   In leads or oils? What old or newer torture
   Must I receive, whose every word deserves
   To taste of thy most worst? Thy tyranny,
   Together working with thy jealousies—
180 Fancies° too weak for boys, too green and idle
   For girls of nine—O think what they have done,
   And then run mad indeed, stark mad; for all
   Thy bygone fooleries were but spices° of it.
   That thou betrayed'st Polixenes,° 'twas nothing.
185 That did but show thee, of a fool,° inconstant,
   And damnable ingrateful. Nor was't much
   Thou wouldst have poisoned good Camillo's°
      honor
   To have him kill a king—poor trespasses,
   More monstrous standing by,° whereof I reckon°
190 The casting forth to crows° thy baby daughter

To be or none, or little,° though a devil
Would have shed water out of fire ere done't.°
Nor is't directly laid to thee the death
Of the young prince,° whose honorable thoughts—
195 Thoughts high° for one so tender°—cleft° the heart
That could conceive a gross and foolish sire°
Blemished° his gracious dam.° This is not, no,
Laid to thy answer.° But the last—O lords,
When I have said,° cry "woe!" The Queen, the
       Queen,
The sweet'st, dear'st creature's dead, and vengeance
200   for't
Not dropped down yet.°
[A LORD   The higher powers forbid!]
PAULINA
I say she's dead. I'll swear't. If word nor oath
Prevail not, go and see. If you can bring
Tincture° or lustre in her lip, her eye,
205 Heat outwardly or breath within, I'll serve you
As I would do the gods. But O thou tyrant,°
Do not repent these things, for they are heavier
Than all thy woes can stir.° Therefore betake° thee
To nothing but despair. A thousand knees,°
210 Ten thousand years together, naked, fasting,
Upon a barren mountain, and still winter
In storm perpetual, could not move the gods
To look that way thou wert.°
[LEONTES   Go on, go on.
Thou canst not speak too much. I have deserved
All tongues to talk their bitt'rest.
A LORD (to Paulina)
215 Say no more.
Howe'er the business goes, you have made fault
I'th' boldness of your speech.]
  PAULINA   I am sorry for't.
All faults I make, when I shall come to know them

164

I do repent. Alas, I have showed too much
220 The rashness of a woman. He is touched°
To th' noble heart. What's gone and what's past
    help
Should be past grief.
(To Leontes)   Do not receive affliction
At my petition.° I beseech you, rather
Let me be punished, that have minded° you
225 Of what you should forget. Now, good my liege,
Sir, royal sir, forgive a foolish woman.
The love I bore your queen—lo, fool again!
I'll speak of her no more, nor of your children.
I'll not remember° you of my own lord,°
230 Who is lost too. Take your patience to you,
And I'll say nothing.

172 **cut my lace**/cut the cords fastening my bodice (i.e., in order for her to breathe) 174 **studied**/devious **hast**/hast thou 175 **flaying**/stripping of skin 180 **Fancies**/imaginings 183 **spices**/tastes, samplings 184 **Polixenes**/King of Bohemia and guest of Leontes, who was accused of having an affair with Queen Hermione 185 **of a fool**/for a fool 187 **Camillo**/the honest counsellor of Leontes and cup-bearer of Polixenes, who was commanded by Leontes to poison Polixenes and refused to do it 189 **standing by**/awaiting **reckon**/count (Paulina now delivers the most dreadful of details that are even worse than the ones mentioned so far.) 190 **casting...crows**/i.e., Leontes had ordered that his new born daughter, Perdita, be taken to the wilderness and left to die 191 **To be...little**/i.e., to live, die, or be as nothing 192 **shed...done't**/i.e., cried tears in the midst of Hell before doing such a thing 194 **prince**/i.e., Mamillius, son of Leontes and Hermione, who died of a broken heart over his mother's misfortune 195 **high**/noble **tender**/young **cleft**/split 196 **sire**/father (i.e., Leontes) 197 **Blemished**/stained **dam**/madam (i.e., mother) 197-198 **This... answer**/i.e., you are not convicted of this crime, nor must you answer for it 199 **said**/reported it 201 **Not...yet**/i.e., not fallen on anyone's head yet 204 **Tincture**/color 206 **thou tyrant**/(She speaks directly to Leontes again.) 208 **woes can stir**/penitences can agitate **betake**/take 209 **knees**/i.e., kneeling in penance 213 **To look...wert**/i.e., to look in your direction 220 **touched**/moved 222-223 **Do not...petition**/i.e., do not suffer because I have prayed that you should 224 **minded**/reminded 229 **remember/remind** **my own lord**/Antigonus, husband of Paulina, who took Perdita into the wilderness and was killed by a bear

Commentary: Paulina's outspoken monologue is both a messenger's report and a bitter, castigating lament. But the actor should be aware that the whole speech is a trick. Hermione, in fact, is not

dead, but stages a ruse and goes into hiding to punish Leontes for all
the wickedness his jealousy has produced. However, not even the
audience must know this. So Paulina's speech must be delivered
with full grief and authenticity. The verse captures her rage. Each
line is delivered as a challenge to Leontes and isolates his meanness
in harsh, torturous images that gradually build to the report of the
Queen's death (lines 198-201). The Lord's comment (lines 215-217)
suggests how far Paulina's "boldness" has gone, and she then pulls
back in self-conscious remorse. Notice how the speech begins in the
white heat of passion ("woe the while!"), goes through a stage of
reckless abandon, and then returns to the more appropriate distance
between a courtier and king. It ends quietly with the word
"nothing." The challenging tone becomes a beseeching one by the
end. But the speech has been strong enough to make the haughty
King Leontes totally transform into a penitent.

BREECHES PARTS

Regardless of their gender, the great characters and speeches of Shakespeare have always attracted intrepid performers. The practice of "breeches parts"—the playing of youthful, romantic heroes by "personality" actresses—was established during the English Restoration by the glamorous Nell Gwynn and others, and quickly expanded to include tragic roles. Charlotte Cushman, Sarah Bernhardt, Dame Judith Anderson, and, most recently at the New York Public Shakespeare Festival, Diane Venora are among the bright luminaries who have responded to the great challenges in Shakespeare's male roles. We invite you to join this noble tradition.

AS YOU LIKE IT

Jaques

*Act 2, Scene 7. Forest of Arden. Jaques delivers this
"set speech" to an onstage audience of the banished
Duke Senior and his fellow exiles. The young Orlando
has just barged in on the group and has exited to fetch
his old retainer Adam. The incident prompts Jaques's
commentary.*

[DUKE SENIOR
    Thou seest we are not all alone unhappy.
    This wide and universal theatre
    Presents more woeful pageants than the scene
    Wherein we play in.]
JAQUES   All the world's a stage,
140 And all the men and women merely players.
    They have their exits and their entrances,
    And one man in his time plays many parts,
    His acts being seven ages. At first the infant,
    Mewling° and puking in the nurse's arms.
145 Then the whining schoolboy with his satchel
    And shining morning face, creeping like snail
    Unwillingly to school. And then the lover,
    Sighing like furnace, with a woeful ballad
    Made to his mistress' eyebrow. Then, a soldier,
150 Full of strange oaths, and bearded like the pard,°
    Jealous in honor, sudden, and quick in quarrel,
    Seeking the bubble° reputation
    Even in the cannon's mouth. And then the justice,
    In fair round belly with good capon lined,°
155 With eyes severe and beard of formal cut,
    Full of wise saws° and modern° instances;
    And so he plays his part. The sixth age shifts
    Into the lean and slippered pantaloon,°

With spectacles on nose and pouch on side,
160 His youthful hose,° well saved, a world too wide
For his shrunk shank,° and his big, manly voice,
Turning again toward childish treble, pipes
And whistles in his sound. Last scene of all,
That ends this strange, eventful history,
165 Is second childishness and mere° oblivion,
Sans° teeth, sans eyes, sans taste, sans everything.
(Enter Orlando bearing Adam)

144 **Mewling**/crying 150 **pard**/leopard (Lat., *pardus*) 152 **bubble**/empty
and insubstantial 154 **with...lined**/allusion to the practice of bribing a
judge with a capon (chicken) 156 **saws**/sayings **modern**/everyday 158
pantaloon/foolish old man (of Italian *commedia dell'arte*) 160 **hose**/
stockings 161 **shrunk shank**/thin ankles 165 **mere**/utter 166 **Sans**/
without (Fr.) (Note how it's repetition gives a funereal bell-tolling quality to
the final line.)

Commentary: Jaques (pronounced *Ja'kis*) is a world weary,
melancholic wit. A haughty lord seldom given to laughter, he is
well-seasoned in the ways of human vanity. A cynic and loner with
no major function in the play except to stand in dark contrast to the
green world of Arden, Jaques is a master of words and stories. And
this speech, like other things he says, is listened to carefully. The
monologue is typical of the way Shakespeare uses the image of the
"theatre" as an analogy for the world. In one speech of seven
distinct phases, we watch an imaginary character literally grow,
age and decline into "oblivion." Then Orlando enters with Adam to
illustrate! Jaques uses strong, actable images that can be physically
represented. Words like "mewling," "puking," "whining" and
"shining" have extraordinary sound qualities. There is a resonant
use of antithesis: entrances/exits; world too wide/shrunk shank.
Notice, finally, how the whole speech slows down at "Last scene of
all" (line 163), coming to a breathless halt at "everything."

HAMLET

Hamlet

*Act 3, Scene 1.   Elsinore castle.   With Claudius and
Polonius hidden from view, Hamlet enters to continue
his reflections on action and inaction, being and non-
being.   This famous soliloquy is on a higher
philosophical and metaphysical plane than all his
others.   It comes halfway in the play.*

HAMLET

55   To be, or not to be; that is the question:
     Whether 'tis nobler in the mind to suffer
     The slings and arrows of outrageous° fortune,
     Or to take arms against a sea of troubles,
     And, by opposing, end them. To die, to sleep—
60   No more°—and by a sleep to say we end
     The heartache and the thousand natural shocks
     That flesh is heir to—'tis a consummation°
     Devoutly to be wished. To die, to sleep.—
     To sleep, perchance° to dream. Ay, there's the rub,°
65   For in that sleep of death what dreams may come
     When we have shuffled off° this mortal coil°
     Must give us pause.° There's the respect°
     That makes calamity° of so long life,
     For who would bear the whips and scorns of time,
70   Th'oppressor's wrong, the proud man's
        contumely,°
     The pangs of disprized° love, the law's delay,
     The insolence of office, and the spurns
     That patient merit of th'unworthy takes,
     When he himself might his quietus° make
75   With a bare bodkin?° Who would these fardels°
        bear,
     To grunt and sweat under a weary life,

But that the dread of something after death,
The undiscovered country from whose bourn°
No traveller returns, puzzles° the will,
80 And makes us rather bear those ills we have
Than fly to others that we know not of?
Thus conscience° does make cowards of us all,
And thus the native hue° of resolution
Is sicklied o'er with the pale cast° of thought,
85 And enterprises of great pitch° and moment°
With this regard their currents° turn awry,
And lose the name of action.

57 **outrageous**/unrestrained, excessive 60 **No more**/(the isolation of the phrase between pauses should be noted and used) 62 **consummation**/end 64 **perchance**/perhaps **rub**/problem, impediment 66 **shuffled off**/freed ourselves of **mortal coil**/life's tensions, upheavals 67 **pause**/moment to consider **respect**/consideration 68 **calamity**/ distress, misery 70 **contumely**/contempt 71 **disprized**/scorned 74 **quietus**/settling of an account 75 **bare bodkin**/naked dagger **fardels**/burdens 78 **bourn**/boundary, region 79 **puzzles**/bewilders 82 **conscience**/being, self-consciousness 83 **native hue**/complexion 84 **sicklied...cast**/covered with a faint hue 85 **pitch**/loftiness, in Q2 *pith* or gravity **moment**/cause 86 **currents**/sense of direction

Commentary: This is perhaps Hamlet's greatest interior monologue. Weighing the infinitives "To be or not to be," Hamlet starts this speech with abstractions. Positive and negative values—being and nonbeing—are pitted against each other. Unlike in his previous soliloquies, the personal "I" is never mentioned. Hamlet talks about himself in the abstract, giving an almost clinical diagnosis of his problem. The theme of the soliloquy is destruction and suicide. Arriving at a decision is the intention of the speech. Much less intense and more general than the previous "O what a rogue and peasant slave am I" soliloquy, Hamlet is able to go into elaborate detail about death because he is so focused on its image. The speech has such celebrated perfection partly because it builds so evenly and progressively towards its final word—action. It is also Hamlet's greatest moment in the role of thinker. From this point on in the play he enters the role of doer.

HENRY IV, Part 2

Rumor

Induction. The play begins with Rumor, dressed in a grotesque robe painted full of tongues. The character recounts the closing action of the first part of Henry IV *and sets the stage for this second part. This is the character's only appearance.*

RUMOR

Open your ears; for which of you will stop
The vent° of hearing when loud Rumor speaks?
I from the orient to the drooping west,°
Making the wind my post-horse,° still° unfold
5   The acts° commencèd on this ball of earth.°
Upon my tongues continual slanders ride,
The which in every language I pronounce,
Stuffing the ears of men with false reports.
I speak of peace, while covert° enmity
10 Under the smile of safety wounds the world;
And who but Rumor, who but only I,
Make fearful musters° and prepared defence
Whiles the big° year, swoll'n with some other
   griefs,
Is thought with child by the stern tyrant war,
15 And no such matter?° Rumor is a pipe
Blown by surmises,° Jealousy's conjectures,°
And of so easy and so plain a stop°
That the blunt monster with uncounted heads,
The still-discordant wav'ring multitude,
20 Can play upon it. But what need I thus
My well-known body to anatomize°
Among my household? Why is Rumor here?
I run before King Harry's victory,
Who in a bloody field by Shrewsbury
25 Hath beaten down young Hotspur and his troops,

Quenching the flame of bold rebellion
Even with the rebels' blood. But what mean I
To speak so true at first?° My office is
To noise abroad° that Harry Monmouth° fell
30 Under the wrath of noble Hotspur's sword,
And that the King before the Douglas' rage
Stooped his anointed head as low as death.
This have I rumored through the peasant towns
Between that royal field of Shrewsbury
35 And this° worm-eaten hold of raggèd stone,
Where Hotspur's father, old Northumberland,
Lies crafty-sick. The posts° come tiring° on,
And not a man of them brings other news
Than they have learnt of me. From Rumor's
  tongues
40 They bring smooth comforts false, worse than true
  wrongs.

2 **vent**/opening, freedom from restraint 3 **I...west**/i.e., from sunrise to
sunset 4 **post-horse**/mail carrier **still**/continually, without stop 5 **acts**/
actions (theatrical meaning, i.e., earlier acts of *Henry IV*) **ball of earth**/
globe 9 **covert**/secret 12 **musters**/gathering of an army 13 **big**/ pregnant
15 **no such matter**/i.e., not at all true 16 **surmises**/speculations
conjectures/evil suspicions 17 **stop**/finger hole that alters a pipe's pitch
and sound 21 **anatomize**/lay bare, interpret 27-28 **But...first?**/i.e., "but
why am I telling you the truth when I should be spreading lies?" 29 **noise
abroad**/spread rumors **Harry Monmouth**/Prince Harry, the victor over
Hotspur 35 **this**/the setting (character is probably indicating the stage set)
37 **posts**/reports **tiring**/feeding ravenously

Commentary: Rumor's soliloquy is pure exposition and mood
setting. It starts in motion the string of lies and deceits in the play
to follow. Rumor doesn't have much in the way of character. What
he/she does have is an arsenal of attention-grabbing devices.
"Open your ears," immediately commands the audience's attention,
as it is meant to do. An allegorical figure in a costume covered in
tongues (perhaps a monster because rumors are ugly), Rumor speaks
in an elaborate rhetorical style that is rich with similes and
metaphors: "Rumor is a pipe/Blown by surmises, Jealousy's
conjectures," etc. At line 22 Rumor finally gets down to business and
provides the audience with a resumé of action since the close of

Henry IV, Part 1. Because Rumor is a bearer of confused and conflicting reports ("Upon my tongues continual slanders ride"), the character probably projects a crafty, malicious villainy to match his/her rumor-mongering calumny.

HENRY IV, Part 2

Epilogue

Epilogue. The stage has been cleared. The epilogue is spoken by a dancer to the audience.

EPILOGUE
First my fear,° then my curtsy,° last my speech.

    My fear is your displeasure;° my curtsy, my duty; and my speech to beg your pardons. If you look for a good speech now, you undo° me; for what I have
5 to say is of mine own making,° and what indeed I should say will, I doubt, prove mine own marring.° But to the purpose, and so to the venture. Be it known to you, as it is very well, I was lately here in the end of a displeasing play,° to pray your patience
10 for it, and to promise you a better. I did mean indeed to pay you with this; which, if like an ill venture° it come unluckily home,° I break,° and you, my gentle creditors, lose. Here I promised you I would be, and here I commit my body to your
15 mercies. Bate° me some, and I will pay you some, and, as most debtors do, promise you infinitely.

    If my tongue cannot entreat you to acquit° me, will you command me to use my legs? And yet that were but light payment, to dance out of your
20 debt. But a good conscience will make any possible satisfaction, and so would I. All the gentlewomen here have forgiven me; if the gentlemen will not, then the gentlemen do not agree with the gentlewomen, which was never seen before in such an
25 assembly.

    One word more, I beseech you. If you be not too much cloyed° with fat meat, our humble author

will continue the story with Sir John in it, and
make you merry with fair Katherine of France;°
30 where, for anything° I know, Falstaff shall die of a
sweat°—unless already a be killed with your hard
opinions. For Oldcastle° died a martyr,° and this is
not the man. My tongue is weary; when my legs
are too, I will bid you good night, and so kneel
35 down before you—but, indeed, to pray for the
Queen.
(He dances, then kneels for applause.   Exit.)

1 **fear**/(perhaps pretended stagefright) **curtsy**/bow, courtesy 2 **My...
displeasure**/i.e., that you did not like the play or a part of it 4 **undo**/ruin 5
mine own making/i.e., actor's speech and not the playwright's   6
marring/spoiling (pun on "making") 9 **displeasing play**/(presumably a
previous, but unnamed, play in the same theatre booed by the audience)
12 **venture**/business venture **unluckily home**/prove disastrous **break**/
go bankrupt 15 **Bate**/quarrel or debate (also a wordplay on *bait*, to hurl
abuse or attack with dogs) 17 **acquit**/prove innocent and set free 27
cloyed/satiated, full 27-29 **author...France**/i.e., highlights of *Henry V* 30
anything/all 31 **sweat**/the sweating plague 32 **Oldcastle**/Sir John
Oldcastle, the character upon whom Shakespeare based Falstaff
martyr/(or so some sources say)

Commentary: In strong contrast to the sneering Induction spoken
by Rumor, the Epilogue of *Henry IV* has a festive quality. The
former character was all tongues, the latter is both tongue and legs.
The speech dances with simple merry things: nonsense sayings and
doggerel. Its chief purpose is to put the audience in a good mood,
especially after they have just seen a popular character like
Falstaff literally put down. At the end of the speech, Epilogue
kneels, reminding us of Falstaff's forced kneeling to King Harry. But
Epilogue's prayer is to Queen Elizabeth. It's likely that the line,
"for what I have to say is of mine own making," shows that the
clown speeches of Shakespeare allowed for improvisations by the
actor. The words are only a pretext for a little cabaret turn while
the audience leaves the theatre. And it also prepares for the play
they will next see; a kind of coming attractions for *Henry V*.

HENRY V

Prologue

Prologue. Empty stage. The Chorus enters as Prologue to set both the scene of the play's action and the audience's imagination to work.

CHORUS

O for a Muse of fire,° that would ascend
The brightest heaven of invention:°
A kingdom for a stage, princes to act,
And monarchs to behold the swelling scene.°
5   Then should the warlike Harry, like himself,
Assume the port° of Mars, and at his heels,
Leashed in like hounds, should famine, sword, and
      fire
Crouch for employment. But pardon, gentles all,
The flat unraisèd spirits° that hath dared
10 On this unworthy scaffold° to bring forth
So great an object.° Can this cock-pit° hold
The vasty fields of France? Or may we cram
Within this wooden O° the very casques°
That did affright the air at Agincourt°?
15 O pardon: since a crookèd figure may
Attest in little place a million,°
And let us, ciphers° to this great account,
On your imaginary forces work.
Suppose within the girdle° of these walls
20 Are now confined two mighty monarchies,°
Whose high uprearèd and abutting fronts°
The perilous narrow ocean° parts asunder.
Piece out our imperfections° with your thoughts:
Into a thousand parts divide one man,
25 And make imaginary puissance.°
Think, when we talk of horses, that you see them,
Printing° their proud hoofs i'th' receiving earth;

For 'tis your thoughts that now must deck° our
  kings,
Carry them here and there, jumping o'er times,°
30   Turning th'accomplishment of many years
Into an hourglass—for the which supply,
Admit me Chorus to this history,°
Who Prologue-like your humble patience pray
Gently to hear, kindly to judge, our play.

1 fire/a shot or volley 2 invention/poetic invention 1-4 O...scene/i.e., if this play could rise above poetic limitations then this limited stage would be a genuine kingdom and real princes and monarchs would replace mere actors 6 port/visage 9 flat unraisèd spirits/dull aspiring actors 10 scaffold/raised stage 11 object/objective, presentation cock-pit/theatre (meaning had been transferred from gaming bird arena to the theatre) 13 wooden O/circular theatre built of wood, Elizabethan playhouse casques/helmets 14 Agincourt/French city that is scene of decisive English victory in *Henry V* 15-16 since...million/a zero or low sum in place of a million; i.e., one actor for many armies 17 ciphers/nonentities 19 girdle/belt, circuit 20 monarchies/i.e., England and France 21 fronts/cliff frontiers 22 ocean/i.e., English Channel 23 imperfections/i.e., that which the stage cannot represent 25 puissance/troops, strength 27 Printing/stamping, implanting 28 deck/dress 29 times/i.e., the exigencies of plot, time and place 31-32 for...history/i.e., the Chorus will act as guide in the story and narrate unrepresented events before each new act

Commentary: This expository soliloquy is aimed directly at the audience. It includes some of Shakespeare's most memorable verse lines and is one of his great homages to the power of the theatre. Like Rumor in *Henry IV, Part 2*, Prologue tells the audience what it will see and hear in the action ahead. The character previews things to come. Unlike Rumor's monologue, Prologue's soliloquy is much more glorious because *Henry V* is a more glorious and heightened play. The monologue is given epic, Homeric dimensions: "Then should the warlike Harry, like himself,/Assume the port of Mars," etc. "Ascend" is truly an operative word in this speech. For words and images attain a height of poetry here that is rare. Prologue is most accomplished and inventive when telling an audience how to view the world of the stage: "Into a thousand parts divide one man;" "Think, when we talk of horses, that you see them." The imaginative conviction that it takes to watch and listen to drama are here addressed: the audience must merge with the actor into a common experience of fictional event.

HENRY V

Chorus

Act 3. The Chorus begins each of the five acts of Henry V.

CHORUS
    Thus with imagined wing° our swift scene flies
    In motion of no less celerity°
    Than that of thought. Suppose that you have seen
    The well-appointed° king at Dover pier°
5   Embark his royalty,° and his brave fleet
    With silken streamers the young Phoebus°
       fanning.
    Play with your fancies,° and in them behold
    Upon the hempen tackle° ship-boys climbing;
    Hear the shrill whistle, which doth order give
10 To sounds confused; behold the threaden sails,
    Borne with th'invisible and creeping wind,
    Draw the huge bottoms° through the furrowed sea,
    Breasting the lofty surge. O do but think
    You stand upon the rivage° and behold
15 A city° on th'inconstant billows dancing—
    For so appears this fleet majestical,
    Holding due course to Harfleur.° Follow, follow!
    Grapple your minds to sternage° of this navy,
    And leave your England, as dead midnight still,
20 Guarded with grandsires, babies, and old women,
    Either past or not arrived to pith and puissance.°
    For who is he, whose chin is but enriched
    With one appearing hair, that will not follow
    These culled and choice-drawn° cavaliers to
       France?
25 Work, work your thoughts, and therein see a siege.
    Behold the ordnance° on their carriages,

With fatal mouths gaping on girded° Harfleur.
Suppose th'ambassador from the French comes
  back,
Tells Harry that the King doth offer him
30 Catherine his daughter, and with her, to dowry,°
Some petty and unprofitable dukedoms.
The offer likes not, and the nimble gunner
With linstock° now the devilish cannon touches,
(Alarum, and chambers go off)
35 And down goes all before them. Still be kind,
And eke out° our performance with your mind.

1 **imagined wing**/flights of imagination 2 **celerity**/speed 4 **well-appointed**/well armed **Dover pier**/i.e., embarkation point for France (earlier the Prologue had fixed this action at Southampton, causing a discrepancy in the text) 5 **royalty**/nobles 6 **Phoebus**/sun god who controls winds 7 **fancies**/imaginations 8 **tackle**/ropes, lines 12 **bottoms**/ ships' hulls 14 **rivage**/shore 15 **city**/i.e., fleet 17 **Harfleur**/French port at the mouth of Seine 18 **sternage**/sterns 21 **pith and puissance**/strength and battle age 24 **culled and choice-drawn**/select, cream of the crop 26 **ordnance**/cannons, guns 27 **girded**/fortified 30 **to dowry**/added to her dowry 33 **linstock**/torch 35 **eke out**/supplement, draw out

Commentary: The Chorus, who delivered the Prologue, continues his/her narrative soliloquies by again provoking the audiences' imagination. Here the character gives us a bird's eye view, as if from on high, of the English preparations and departure for France. The intention of the Chorus is to have the audience imagine the transitions between acts, especially the massive movements of troops from one country to another. The effect is cinematic and the words convey sound and movement.

HENRY V

Boy

Act 3, Scene 2. France. Battle of Harfleur. A boy, servant to the three buffoons Nym, Bardolph and Pistol, stops to address the audience. This is a moment of comic relief from the fighting.

BOY

As young as I am, I have observed° these three
30 swashers.° I am boy° to them all three, but all they
three, though they should serve me, could not be
man° to me, for indeed three such antics° do not
amount to a man. For Bardolph, he is white-
livered° and red-faced—by the means whereof a
35 faces it out,° but fights not. For Pistol, he hath a
killing tongue° and a quiet sword—by the means
whereof a breaks words,° and keeps whole
weapons. For Nim, he hath heard that men of few
words are the best men, and therefore he scorns to
40 say his prayers, lest a should be thought a coward.
But his few bad words are matched with as few
good deeds—for a never broke any man's head but
his own, and that was against a post, when he was
drunk. They will steal anything, and call it
45 "purchase." Bardolph stole a lute case,° bore it
twelve leagues, and sold it for three halfpence.
Nim and Bardolph are sworn brothers in filching,°
and in Calais° they stole a fire shovel.° I knew by
that piece of service the men would carry coals.°
50 They would have me as familiar with men's
pockets° as their gloves or their handkerchiefs—
which makes° much against my manhood,° if I
should take from another's pocket to put into
mine, for it is plain pocketing up° of wrongs. I

181

55   must leave them, and seek some better service.
     Their villainy goes against my weak stomach, and
     therefore I must cast it up.°

29 **observed**/watched and humored   30 **swashers**/swaggerers, idiots
boy/servant   32 **man**/man servant, as much a man   32 **antics**/clowns,
grotesque buffoons   33-34 **white-livered**/cowardly, i.e., lilly-livered   34-35
a...out/is brazen only in appearance   36 **killing tongue**/words are mightier
than his sword   37 **breaks words**/quarrels   45 **lute case**/(he stole the case
but not the more valuable lute)   47 **filching**/stealing   48 **Calais**/English
port **fire shovel**/i.e., worthless object   49 **carry coals**/i.e., do dirty work   50-
51 **familiar...pockets**/learn to pickpocket (also sexual meaning)   52
makes/interferes **manhood**/proper development (sexual meaning)   54
pocketing up/receiving   57 **cast it up**/give it up or vomit it up

Commentary: The Boy delivers a soliloquy on the subject of
villainy and gross cowardice. This little set speech is in contrast to
the greater patriotic soliloquies of King Harry where courage and
honor are the themes. Delivered in prose, the speech is rough,
colloquial and rich with puns. But it also imparts observed wisdom
about petty criminality. The Boy's motivation is escape from such
ill use. And, indeed, he becomes physically ill by the end of the
speech as a way of punctuating his dilemma. Exposed to petty
crimes and stupidities, the Boy maintains an innocence and morality
in the midst of his immoral education.

A MIDSUMMER NIGHT'S DREAM

Puck

Act 3, Scene 2. The wood near Athen's at night. Puck has administered Oberon's magic, inducing Titania to fall in love with Bottom, who has been transformed into an ass. He reports the episode to Oberon.

PUCK

    My mistress with a monster is in love.
    Near to her close° and consecrated bower
    While she was in her dull and sleeping hour
    A crew of patches,° rude mechanicals°
10 That work for bread upon Athenian stalls,°
    Were met together to rehearse a play
    Intended for great Theseus' nuptial day.°
    The shallowest thickskin° of that barren° sort,
    Who Pyramus presented,° in their sport
15 Forsook° his scene° and entered in a brake,°
    When I did him at this advantage take.
    An ass's nole° I fixèd on his head.
    Anon° his Thisbe° must be answerèd,
    And forth my mimic° comes. When they° him
        spy—
20 As wild geese that the creeping fowler° eye,
    Or russet-pated choughs,° many in sort,
    Rising and cawing at the gun's report,
    Sever themselves and madly sweep the sky—
    So, at his sight, away his fellows fly;
25 And at our stamp° here o'er and o'er one falls.
    He "Murder" cries, and help from Athens calls.
    Their sense thus weak, lost with their fears thus
        strong,
    Made senseless things begin to do them wrong.
    For briers and thorns at their apparel snatch;

30   Some sleeves, some hats—from yielders all things
       catch.
     I led them on in this distracted° fear,
     And left sweet Pyramus translated° there;
     When in that moment, so it came to pass,
     Titania waked and straightway loved an ass.

7 close/hidden 9 patches/fools rude mechanicals/uneducated
workingmen 10 stalls/shops, booths 12 Theseus' nuptial day/(the action
of the play centers around the marriage of Theseus, Duke of Athens, to
Hippolyta, Queen of Amazons) 13 thickskin/blockhead, i.e., Bottom
barren/empty headed, stupid 14 Who Pyramus presented/who acted
Pyramus 15 Forsook/left scene/i.e., the space in which he was playing
brake/thicket of bushes 17 nole/head 18 Anon/immediately Thisbe/i.e.,
other actor playing role in scene 19 mimic/actor they/i.e., the other
mechanicals 20 fowler/bird-catcher 21 chough/bird of crow family 25
stamp/authority 31 distracted/mad 32 translated/transformed

Commentary: Puck's verse is full of rhyming couplets, which add
entertainment to his report and help to vividly dramatize action.
His first line, the only single line ending with a full stop,
summarizes the triumph of his mission. Note how the speech is full
of verbal pursuit and confusion; the verbs are alive with activity.
We can understand why Puck is often played with high energy. As
Oberon's agent provocateur, Puck has been charged to do harm and
mischief. He is not a benign character, even though his tricks have
comic consequences. His role is to manipulate and terrorize. Notice
the mayhem in lines 19-30. The actor who can capture this side of
the character can add substance to an otherwise lightweight role.
Puck's speech also captures the theme of illusion and reality—
"sense" and "senseless"—which dominates the play. Note, also,
the severe disdain that Puck has for Bottom and the other
mechanicals: "The shallowest thickskin of that barren sort." Like
Oberon, Puck favors the use of sibilants to strike his malicious
purpose.

ROMEO AND JULIET

Chorus

Prologue.   The Chorus begins the action on an empty stage, setting the scene and argument for the audience.

CHORUS
Two households, both alike in dignity°
In fair Verona, where we lay our scene,
From ancient° grudge break to new mutiny,°
Where civil blood° makes civil hands° unclean.
5   From forth the fatal loins° of these two foes
A pair of star-crossed° lovers take their life,°
Whose misadventured° piteous overthrows°
Doth with their death bury their parents' strife.
The fearful passage° of their death-marked° love
10   And the continuance of their parents' rage—
Which, but their children's end, naught° could
        remove—
Is now the two-hours' traffic° of our stage;
The which if you with patient ears attend,
What here shall miss, our° toil shall strive to
        mend.

1 **dignity**/rank   3 **ancient**/so old no one seems to know its source
mutiny/violence, quarreling   **civil blood**/passion of civil strife   **civil
hands**/citizens' hands   **loins**/parentage   6 **star-crossed**/fated to disaster,
doomed   **take their life**/commit suicide   7 **misadventured**/unfortunate
overthrows/defeats (by death)   9 **passage**/course   **death-marked**/
doomed   11 **naught**/nothing   12 **traffic**/business   14 **our**/i.e., the players

Commentary: The Chorus speaks a sonnet (14 lines of alternating
end rhymes) in both this instance and later between Acts 1 and 2.
He/She sets the terms of the play: Montagues and Capulets,
dignified houses, have an old blood feud that has recently broken
out in new arguments. The scene is Verona. What the Chorus *never*
tells us is the original cause of the feud. But what he/she does tell
us is that Romeo and Juliet ("star-crossed" by fortune) will suffer as
a result of consequences. They themselves are not tragic, but are

victims caught up in circumstances that are. The chorus also refers
to the play's length—two hours; one of the few references to a
playing time in Shakespeare. The verse here is quite regular and
elegant, forecasting much of the tone of the verse in the play ahead.
"Break" and "bury" are two words whose prominent stresses disrupt
the steady pattern. Both words signal the rupture which is the
subject of the Chorus' speech.

ROMEO AND JULIET

Mercutio

Act 1, Scene 4.   Verona.   The street in front of the Capulet's house at night.   Romeo, Mercutio, Benvolio and a group of maskers are on their way to the Capulet's ball.   Mercutio launches into this bright, fantastical speech to draw Romeo out of his dreamy gloom.

MERCUTIO

O, then I see Queen Mab° hath been with you.°
She is the fairies' midwife,° and she comes
55 In shape no bigger than an agate stone°
On the forefinger of an alderman,°
Drawn with a team of little atomi°
Athwart men's noses as they lie asleep.
Her wagon spokes made of long spinners'° legs;
60 The cover,° of the wings of grasshoppers;
Her traces,° of the moonshine's wat'ry beams;
Her collars, of the smallest spider web;
Her whip, of cricket's bone, the lash of film;°
Her wagoner, a small grey-coated gnat
65 Not half so big as a round little worm
Pricked from the lazy finger of a maid.°
Her chariot is an empty hazelnut
Made by the joiner squirrel° or old grub,°
Time out o' mind the fairies' coachmakers.
70 And in this state° she gallops night by night
Through lovers' brains, and then they dream of
     love;
O'er courtiers' knees, that dream on° curtsies
     straight;°
O'er ladies' lips, who straight on kisses dream,
Which oft the angry Mab with blisters plagues°

75 Because their breaths with sweetmeats tainted are.°
    Sometime she gallops o'er a lawyer's lip,
    And then dreams he of smelling out a suit;°
    And sometime comes she with a tithe-pigs° tail
    Tickling a parson's nose as a lies asleep;
80 Then dreams he of another benefice.°
    Sometime she driveth o'er a soldier's neck,
    And then dreams he of cutting foreign throats,
    Of breaches, ambuscados,° Spanish blades,°
    Of healths° five fathom deep; and then anon
85 Drums in his ear, at which he starts and wakes,
    And being thus frighted, swears a prayer or two,°
    And sleeps again. This is that very Mab
    That plaits the manes of horses in the night,
    And bakes the elf-locks in foul sluttish hairs,°
90 Which once untangled much misfortune bodes.
    This is the hag,° when maids lie on their backs,
    That presses them and learns them first to bear,
    Making them women of good carriage.°
    This is she—
[ROMEO   Peace, peace, Mercutio, peace!
95 Thou talk'st of nothing.]
MERCUTIO   True. I talk of dreams,
    Which are the children of an idle brain,
    Begot of nothing but vain fantasy,°
    Which is as thin of substance as the air,
    And more inconstant than the wind, who woos
    Even now the frozen bosom of the north,
    And, being angered, puffs away from thence,
    Turning his face to the dew-dropping south.

53 **Queen Mab**/fairy queen (Celtic) **been with you**/slept with you
(bawdy) 54 **midwife**/i.e., delivers men's fantasies like births 55 **agate
stone**/common ring gemstone 56 **alderman**/local magistrate 57 **atomi**/
tiny, speck-like creatures 59 **spinners'**/spiders' 60 **cover**/canopy 61
traces/harnesses 63 **film**/gossamer 66 **Pricked...maid**/i.e., lazy maids
were said to have worms breeding in their fingers (besides being grotesque,
the image is also bawdy with "pricked") 68 **squirrel/grub**/both work on the

wood of the nut by gnawing and boring 70 **state**/stately grandeur 72 **on**/of **curtsies straight**/bows 74 **blisters plague**/i.e., sign of venereal disease 75 **Because...are**/(sexual allusion) 77 **smelling out a suit**/discovering a petition that will lead to a fee 78 **tithe-pig**/part of a parson's yearly dues 80 **benefice**/income 83 **ambuscados**/ambushes **blades**/Toledo swords 84 **healths**/toasts 86 **swears...two**/to ward off evil 89 **bakes...hairs**/matts the hairs of foul sluts 91 **hag**/witch or evil spirit (produces pain of childbirth) 93 **carriage**/bearing (pun on "bear") 97 **fantasy**/fancy

Commentary: A showy set speech—"a vain fantasy"—that is full of dazzling images and jewel-like miniatures, Mercutio's soliloquy bears little relation to the action. It is speech-making for its own sake. It is meant to be an entertaining divertissement that captures the carnival atmosphere of the scene. This is not a monologue to rush through. Delicacy is woven into each image and artfulness of delivery lurks behind each phrase. Note the heavy use of sibilants in the verse: "O'er courtiers' knees, that dream on curtsies straight;/O'er ladies' lips, who straight on kisses dream." The "s" sounds prevent the actor from rushing past the details. This is a speech where all the exquisite details must be imagined and heard. Mercutio is presenting a pageant-like fantasia. He mixes child-like dreams, bawdy sexuality and a darker grotesque element (see lines 83-89) that gradually transform the speech into a nightmare. In a way, the whole Queen Mab speech resembles the movement of the play from innocence to the macabre. The actor must remember that Mercutio is an agile character physically. So a speech like this naturally lends itself to all manner of performance.

SELECTED BIBLIOGRAPHY
OF TITLES IN PRINT

Barton, John. *Playing Shakespeare*. London and New York: Methuen, 1984. Possibly the best book available on this subject, but most useful when read in conjunction with seeing the video films upon which it is based.

Brown, John Russell. *Discovering Shakespeare: A New Guide to the Plays*. London: Macmillan, 1981. An excellent short introduction to Shakespeare's plays in the theatre.

_____. *Shakespeare's Dramatic Style*. London: Heinemann, 1970. Explores the working of the text in *Romeo and Juliet, As you Like It, Julius Caesar, Twelfth Night* and *Macbeth*.

Goldman, Michael. *Acting and Action in Shakespearean Tragedy*. Princeton, NJ: Princeton University Press, 1985. Academic in tone, useful nonetheless for its sometimes penetrating ideas.

Joseph, Bertram. *Acting Shakespeare*. New York: Theatre Arts Books, 1960. One of the first books to treat the subject of acting Shakespeare, there are still useful ideas here.

_____. *A Shakespeare Workbook (Two Volumes)*. New York: Theatre Arts Books, 1980. Goes through a number of plays and speeches, working through specific points of text.

MacLeish, Kenneth. *Longman Guide to Shakespeare's Characters*. London: Longman, 1985. A fun and usable Who's Who of Shakespeare. Best for exploring character.

OTHER VALUABLE TEXTS IN PRINT

Berry, Cicely. *The Actor and His Text*. London, 1987.

Brubaker, E.S. *Shakespeare Aloud: A Guide to His Verse on Stage*. Pennsylvania, 1976.

Cook, Judith. *Shakespeare's Players*. London, 1983.

David, Richard. *Shakespeare in the Theatre*. London, 1978.

Frye, Northrop. *Northrop Frye on Shakespeare*. New Haven and London, 1986.

Gibson, William. *Shakespeare's Game*. New York, 1978.

Granville-Barker, Harley. *Prefaces to Shakespeare, Volume I*. New Jersey, 1946.

Granville-Barker, Harley. *Prefaces to Shakespeare, Volume II*. New Jersey, 1947.

Gurr, Andrew. *The Shakespearean Stage, 1574-1642*. Cambridge, 1980.

Kott, Jan. *Shakespeare Our Contemporary*. New York, 1964.

Magee, Judy. *You Don't Have To Be British To Do Shakespeare*. New York, 1985.

Onions, C.T. *A Shakespeare Glossary*. Oxford, 1986.

Sher, Antony. *Year of the King*. New York, 1987.

Spurgeon, Caroline. *Shakespeare's Imagery and What It Tells Us*. Cambridge, 1935.

Styan, J.L. *Shakespeare's Stagecraft*. Cambridge, 1967.

* * *

Although there are many editions of Shakespeare's plays available, the best are perhaps the recently published *Complete Plays* (Oxford University Press, 1986) and the separate editions published by Methuen (Arden Series), Penguin, and Signet. All have excellent notes. A fine standard edition is also the much used *Riverside Shakespeare*.

The books we have cited are generally available at first-rate general bookshops, college bookshops, and we trust at all performing arts bookshops. They may all be ordered by mail from Applause Theatre Books, 211 West 71 Street, New York, NY 10023, (212) 595-4735.

SHAKESCENES: SHAKESPEARE FOR TWO

The Shakespeare Scenebook

EDITED AND WITH AN INTRODUCTION
BY JOHN RUSSELL BROWN

Thirty-five scenes are presented in newly edited texts, with notes which clarify meanings, topical references, puns, ambiguities, etc. Each scene has been chosen for its independent life requiring only the simplest of stage properties and the barest of spaces. A brief description of characters and situation prefaces each scene and is followed by a commentary which discusses its major acting challenges and opportunities.

paper ∎ ISBN 1-55783-049-5